100 ANIMALS

NICK GARBUTT

with
Mike Unwin

Bradt

Reprinted April 2008
First published October 2007
Bradt Travel Guides Ltd
23 High Street, Chalfont St Peter, Bucks SL9 9QE, England
www.bradtguides.com
Published in the USA by The Globe Pequot Press Inc, 246 Goose Lane,
PO Box 480, Guilford, Connecticut 06475-0480

Editorial Project Manager: Emma Thomson
Picture Researcher: Daniel Austin

Designed and formatted by Artinfusion
Printed and bound in Italy by Printer Trento

100 Animals to See Before They Die
ISBN-10: 1 84162 236 2
ISBN-13: 978 1 84162 236 1

100 Animals to Save Before They Die
ISBN-10: 1 84162 256 7
ISBN-13: 978 1 84162 256 9

British Library Cataloguing in Publication Data
A catalogue record for this book is available from the British Library

Foreword

Extinction is for ever. It's an absolute, like death, so when the idea came up to publish a book using the rankings of the recently-announced EDGE list I argued that mammals that breed well in captivity, such as tigers and orang-utans, should not be included. They may become extinct in the wild, perhaps, but we could always see them in zoos. Nick Garbutt argued persuasively that this doesn't count; that to see a tiger in its natural habitat is as spine-tingling as any travel experience available to us. That, he said, was surely what conservation – and Bradt Travel Guides – are all about. Yes, Nick, I agree.

Bradt has been advising travellers on seeing animals in their natural surroundings since 1977, when our first guidebook to Africa gave details of visiting the yet-to-be-habituated mountain gorillas of Rwanda and Zaire. If the animal you are observing is an endangered species it adds an emotional factor that you can never find in a zoo. The experience is unforgettable, even if you only glimpsed the animal. And to understand why its future is uncertain you need to see where it lives and appreciate – and worry about – the human pressures that have put it at risk. Then, once you've developed this emotional link, you will want to know how you can help.

And if I was cynical about the 'before they die' aspect of this book when we first discussed it, the possible extinction of the Yangtze river dolphin during the course of writing gave me a jolt. If this mammal has gone, it's gone. Full stop. How many other species will have joined it before the decade is out?

Hilary Bradt

Contents

◀ The solitary life of a polar bear epitomises the bleak, austere expanses of the High Arctic.

Introduction

Life on Earth has been around rather a long time: 3.75 billion years, give or take. From humble, single-celled beginnings an immense complexity and abundance has blossomed. Yet the number of species alive today is but a fraction of the total that has ever existed. Since the dawn of life, countless species have come and gone. In fact more than 99.9% are now extinct. And their demise had nothing to do with us.

Extinction is an entirely natural process that has taken place throughout history. Think about it for a moment: we do not share this planet with dinosaurs, trilobites or any of the other weird and wonderful life forms we know from the fossil record. Why? Because they are extinct. As sure as every individual organism that lives will die, every species that evolves will eventually die out. Some disappear relatively quickly; others persist for much longer. Most species' tenure on Earth lasts for between one and ten million years, with vertebrates like mammals generally at the shorter end of this range.

Extinction, however, is not a consistent phenomenon. The history of life has seen long periods of stability followed by much more turbulent passages, where extinctions have occurred at catastrophic levels. There have been five of these so-called mass extinction events, in which up to 95% of known species have disappeared in – geologically speaking – the blink of an eye. The last of these took place around 65 million years ago when an asteroid collided with Earth, leading to massive climate change and the disappearance of the dinosaurs.

Yet these events are not solely destructive, since the extinction of one species heralds new opportunities for others. Take the demise of the dinosaurs. The 'terrible lizards' dominated life on Earth for over 100 million years, and for most of this time they shared the planet with a group of small, hairy, rather insignificant creatures – the early mammals – that hid themselves away in the shadows. With the dinosaurs gone, this new cast of characters grabbed centre stage and within the next 20–25 million years a wealth of newcomers evolved to fill the gaps. This evolutionary lineage produced all the mammals we see today, including ourselves. It is sobering to think that, had there been no asteroid impact, dinosaurs might still rule the roost

Extinct lemur skull: *In less than 2,000 years, man has eliminated at least 17 giant lemur species from Madagascar.* ▶

and we would never have existed. But from massive destruction came today's glorious diversity.

And it is this diversity that we, human beings, are now threatening. This book describes 100 species of mammal that are in imminent danger of disappearing forever. The circumstances may vary but the root cause in every case is clear: *Homo sapiens*. And this is just the tip of the iceberg. The list could easily have numbered 500, and for every 500 endangered mammals, there are at least 500 endangered birds, reptiles, amphibians, fish and invertebrates. The inescapable truth is staggering: through our actions – direct persecution or habitat destruction – we are currently causing the sixth mass extinction event. Humankind is the greatest catastrophic agent the Earth has experienced in 65 million years.

Human induced extinctions are nothing new. The development and spread of *Homo sapiens* over the past 150,000 or so years has spelt doom for other organisms worldwide. In the Americas 12–10 thousand years ago there were dramatic waves of extinction when the first colonising humans hunted out giant mammals such as woolly mammoths and sabre-toothed tigers. Similarly, the Polynesians ransacked one island group after another as they colonised the Pacific. Numerous more recent examples make for grim reading: the passenger pigeon, Tasmanian wolf and most famously, the dodo, all obliterated in a short period.

▲ **Dodo (reconstruction):** *Is there a more powerful and poignant symbol of man's capacity to exterminate a species?*

So why is what we are doing today so different? The answer is simply one of scale. With rampant technological advance, our capacity for destruction has increased exponentially. If we continue to plunder the world around us at our current rate a quarter of the world's species may well disappear in the next century. This mass extinction is fundamentally different from the five that have gone before. Those were caused by physical factors that were beyond control: asteroid impact, dramatic fluctuation in sea levels and so forth. The current catastrophe is the work of a single insatiable species pursuing its own agenda. Now that we have grasped this, surely we also have the power to alter our actions and stave off the consequences.

Does this matter? If biodiversity was halved, would the Earth be a worse place? The answer is an unequivocal yes. Immeasurably worse. Species do not exist in isolation: they are part of communities, which in turn form environments that join seamlessly together in an ecologically integrated planet. Thus all the world's species interconnect and interact in a complex multitude of tangled networks to produce a healthy living world. Disrupt one and there is a modest ripple of discontent; disrupt many and there is a tidal wave of irreversible decay. We are part of this interconnectivity, not, in some superior way, divorced from it. By destroying the environments and species around us, we are threatening the life support systems on which all species depend – including our own.

Even though our species is eventually destined for extinction, just like all other species in history, we have both a moral and a practical imperative to protect nature's diversity. If we fail, then we are ultimately hastening our own demise, too.

The Edge of Existence Programme

An alarming proportion of the world's most distinctive mammal species are slipping towards extinction. Indeed, even as this book was going to press, the Yangtze River dolphin – ranked number one EDGE species (see page 31) – was reclassified as probably extinct, after an intensive scientific survey of the Yangtze was unable to find any remaining dolphins in the river. In an attempt to halt this shocking trend, the Zoological Society of London has created an innovative conservation initiative called the EDGE of Existence programme. This programme raises international awareness, implements targeted research and conservation action, and trains aspiring in-country scientists to protect threatened species.

▲ **Yangtze River dolphin:** *Already gone? Recent surveys have failed to find evidence of their continued survival.*

▲ **Baby slender loris:** *Man literally holds the future of species like the slender loris in his hand.*

Life on the edge

EDGE stands for Evolutionarily Distinct and Globally Endangered. It is a way of describing species that represent a significant amount of unique evolutionary history and are also under threat. Such species are often extremely unusual in the way they look, live and behave. If they disappear there will be nothing like them left on the planet. Some of these species, such as elephants and pandas, already receive considerable conservation attention, but many others remain poorly understood and neglected. In fact, a staggering 70% of the world's most threatened and evolutionarily distinct mammal species currently receive little or no conservation attention. If these disappear, they will not only take with them a disproportionate amount of biodiversity, but may also significantly reduce the potential for future evolution.

The EDGE of Existence programme combines cutting-edge scientific research with the latest developments in web-based technology to make conservation accessible across a broad spectrum of society. It centres upon an interactive website (*www.edgeofexistence.org*) that provides detailed information on the world's top 100 EDGE mammals and their conservation needs. This website also facilitates fundraising for targeted research and conservation action for ten focal species each year. Supporters can see how their donations make a difference and help to support urgent conservation actions by following the progress of EDGE researchers through blogs, newsletters and video diaries.

EDGE

The majority of the world's neglected EDGE species occur in developing countries, which frequently lack the capacity to protect them. ZSL recognises that only by transferring skills to local people will long-term conservation goals be met. Aspiring in-country scientists, students or rangers receive training in monitoring techniques, community outreach and education through the EDGE Fellows programme. Each EDGE Fellow carries out extensive research into the threats facing a particular species, in conjunction with local organisations and communities. The result is an accessible conservation action plan for that species, a legacy of highly trained professionals to take the plan forward, and an increased capacity in that country for sustainable, long-term conservation.

In summary, the main goals of the EDGE of Existence programme are to:
1 identify the current status of poorly known and possibly extinct EDGE species
2 develop and implement conservation measures for all EDGE species not currently protected
3 support local scientists to research and conserve EDGE species worldwide.

Uniquely valuable

The Earth is now experiencing the greatest mass extinction of species since the end-Cretaceous event, which wiped out the dinosaurs and many other species 65 million years ago. In the last 500 years, human activity has forced more than 800 species to extinction and if present trends continue almost a quarter of the world's mammals will follow over the next century.

With insufficient resources available to arrest this decline, conservation planners are forced to prioritise which species should receive the most protection. Although a range of approaches have been advocated, scientists are increasingly recognising the importance of conserving evolutionarily distinct species in order to safeguard global biodiversity. Since each species has a unique evolutionary history, the extinction of a species that has been evolving independently for a long period of time and has few relatives – such as, for example, the aardvark – would be a greater loss to biodiversity than that of a young species, like the black rat, which originated only recently and has many close relatives. By protecting such evolutionarily distinct species we can ensure that as wide a range of different creatures as possible survive into the future. This will maximise the chances of life being able to adapt to major environmental catastrophes, such as disease or climate change.

Most organisations focus attention on endemic or charismatic species but until recently none has highlighted the most evolutionarily distinct. This was primarily due to a lack of knowledge about evolutionary relationships. Following the recent publication of a mammal 'supertree' – the first complete diagram of the evolutionary relationships between all known living mammals – ZSL scientists have been able to calculate the proportion of unique evolutionary history every mammal species represents.

▲ **Thylacine:** There are no close living relatives of the Tasmanian wolf, or thylacine, that became extinct in 1936.

1   EDGE scores

EDGE RANK   Every EDGE species has been assigned a 'score' that measures both its uniqueness and its conservation status. This is calculated using two criteria:

Evolutionary Distinctiveness (ED)

A species' uniqueness can be measured as an 'Evolutionary Distinctiveness' (ED) score, using a phylogeny, or evolutionary tree. In the example on the right, species A has a higher ED score than either species B or C, since it represents a branch rather than a twig on the tree of life. If species A were to become extinct, there would be no similar species left on the planet and a significant amount of unique evolutionary history would be lost.

Global Endangerment (GE)

A species' Globally Endangered status is measured according to the IUCN Red List of Threatened Species™, the world's most comprehensive assessment of the conservation status of all flora and fauna.

The two scores are then multiplied to produce an overall EDGE score for each species. This represents a mathematical estimate of the loss of evolutionary history per unit time.

EDGE species are those that have an above-average ED score and are threatened with extinction (according to the IUCN Red List). There are currently 521 EDGE mammal species (roughly 12% of all living mammals). Potential EDGE species are those with high ED scores but whose conservation status is unclear.

Eurasia

Eurasia is the largest biogeographical region on earth. It stretches from western Europe to eastern Russia, south to the tropics of the Indian subcontinent and also encompasses most of the Arctic. This vast area covers about a third of the Earth's landmass and takes in all manner of habitats, from open grasslands, deciduous forest and desert, to dense coniferous forests, frozen tundra and the world's highest mountains.

Unsurprisingly, the species diversity within this region is impressive. But its wild areas and biodiversity are under siege. While Eurasia undoubtedly still harbours areas of wilderness that stretch far beyond the horizon – including the great deserts of central Asia and the snow-capped peaks of the Himalayas – it also encompasses the three most densely populated and industrialised areas on Earth: western Europe, India and China. Together these are home to around 70% of the world's 6.6 billion people.

How can the needs and requirements of people be reconciled with those of the natural environment? While conservationists struggle to find the answer, the pressure intensifies. India alone is home to over one billion people, most concentrated along the great Gangetic floodplain. Yet it is still a country where large, charismatic species like elephants, rhinos, bears and tigers find room to survive. But for how much longer?

◀ *Kanha National Park in central India remains one of the best places to see tigers. This young male was seen emerging from the forest late one afternoon*

Wolverine
p21
Northern latitudes:
from Alaska and
Canada to Siberia and
northern Europe.

Onager
p15
Semnan and Fars
Provinces, Iran.

Steppe pika
p22
Central Asian
steppes: Ural
Mountains to
northern
Kazakhstan.

Saiga antelope
p16
Central Asian
steppes: Russia,
Kazakhstan and
northwest
Mongolia.

Bactrian camel
p14
Northwest China;
Gobi Desert,
southwest
Mongolia.

Long-eared jerboa
p29
Xinjiang, northwest
China; Trans Altai
Govi Desert and
Alashan Plateau,
southern Mongolia.

Giant panda
p18
Gansu, Shaanxi
and Sichuan
provinces, China.

Red panda
p20
Eastern Himalayas:
Nepal, northern
India, Bhutan,
Myanmar and
western China.

**Japanese
dormouse**
p17
Honshu, Shikoku
and Kyushu
islands, Japan.

Iberian lynx
p13
Southwest Spain
and southern
Portugal.

Amami rabbit
p22
Amami Oshima
and Tokunoshima
islands, Ryukyu
Archipelago,
Japan.

**Yangtze river
dolphin**
p31
Yangtze River
only, near
mouth; now
feared extinct.

Iceland
Faroe
Islands
Norway
Sweden
Finland
Ireland
UK
Germany
Poland
Belarus
France
Alps
Ukraine
Portugal
Spain
Pyrenees
Italy
Romania
Urals
Russia
Kazakhstan
Uzbekistan
Turkey
Turkmenistan
Syria
Iraq
Iran
Afghanistan
Gobi desert
Mongolia
China
N Korea
S Korea
Japan
*Arabian
Desert*
Pakistan
Saudi Arabia
Oman
Himalayas
Nepal
Ganges
India
Yangtze
Yemen
Sri Lanka

	Desert
	Taiga (coniferous forest)
	Temperate forest
	Steppe (grass, brush and thicket)
	Dry tropical scrub and forest
	Woodland savanna
	Tropical rainforest
	Chaparral
	Mountains
	Tundra

Takin
p29
Eastern Himalayas,
from India into
western China.

Tiger
p32
Scattered across
southern and
eastern Asia from
India to Sumatra;
northeast to
eastern Siberia.

Snow leopard
p28
Mountains of
central Asia, from
western Himalayas
to southern
Mongolia, especially
Tibet.

Sloth bear
p23
Scattered across
Indian
subcontinent:
India, Nepal,
Bhutan,
Bangladesh
and Sri Lanka.

Slender loris
p17
Confined to
Sri Lanka.

**Ganges river
dolphin**
p30
Ganges-
Brahmaputra-
Meghna and
Karnaphuli-Sangu
river systems,
Bangladesh and
India; Karnali river,
west Nepal.

Indian rhinoceros
p26
Southwest Nepal
and northeast
India, especially
Kaziranga
National Park.

0   500k 1000 1500 2000 2500 3000 km
0   500   1000   2000 miles

Iberian lynx

Lynx pardinus

Head/body: 85–110cm
Weight: up to 13kg (males)
up to 9.5kg (females)

WHERE TO SEE IT

Two places offer a reasonable chance of seeing an Iberian lynx, provided you

make a concentrated effort over several days: Sierra de Andújar in Sierra Morena and Cota Doñana National Park in Andulacia. Try visiting Coto Doñana in September when conditions are dry and the lynxes are more likely to visit areas with remaining freshwater resources. They generally become active around dusk. Wildlife tour companies in Spain, UK and elsewhere organise trips. Details at: www.lynxexsitu.es

THREATS

The lynx's range has been heavily reduced by the loss of its habitat. Its numbers have also been severely affected by a population crash in rabbits, its principal food, following the introduction of the myxomatosis virus in the 1950s and a subsequent new disease called viral haemorrhagic pneumonia. Other serious threats include illegal hunting, accidental deaths in traps and road kills.

133
EDGE RANK

Vanishing cat

This elegant predator looks like a large, lanky domestic cat with tufted ears and a ruff around the cheeks. It is effectively a smaller, spottier version of the Eurasian lynx, and sports the same characteristic bobbed tail and long, powerful legs.

The Iberian lynx is restricted to Mediterranean oak forest, and a surrounding mosaic of scrub, thickets and meadows. Historically it was widespread throughout the Iberian peninsula and the south of France, but it has since been reduced to a handful of isolated populations scattered across suitable habitat in central and southwestern Spain and the Algarve region of Portugal.

Today this is the most threatened cat species in the world, with perhaps no more than 150 animals left in the wild. Its population is divided between two main regions: Cota Doñana (with 30%) and Andújar-Cardeña (with 70%). Between them these support no more than 30–35 breeding females.

Bunny mugger

Like many smaller cats, the Iberian lynx is a creature of the shadows, emerging to hunt by twilight and under cover of darkness. Males and females live separate lives and get together only in January and February to mate.

Rabbits top the menu – one per day being the average requirement. This diet evolved to reduce competition with the Eurasian lynx, which targets bigger prey such as roe deer, although today the ranges of the two species no longer overlap. When needs must, however, the Iberian lynx is more than capable of taking small deer, and may also turn its sights on birds such as ducks and partridges.

Females reach sexual maturity at one year but do not breed until they've established a territory of

their own. They select a den in a thicket or hollow tree and give birth in the spring (March to April) to a litter of two or three. The kittens are weaned at eight months, but stay with their mothers until around 20 months.

Bactrian camel

Camelus ferus

Head/body length: 225–345cm
Height at hump: 180–230cm
Tail length: 35–55cm; Weight: 450–650kg

One hump or two?

Few animals look more improbable than a camel. The Bactrian is the two-humped version of its one-humped cousin, the dromedary. Unlike the dromedary, however, a few Bactrian camels still survive in the wild.

Wild Bactrian camels are smaller than their domestic counterparts and have a number of special features for desert survival. Their thick, shaggy fur can cope with winter temperatures of −40° but peels away in chunks during the hot summer. During sandstorms they can close their nostrils and use their double row of long eyelashes to keep sand out of their eyes. The two large toes on each foot spread wide to help them walk across shifting sand.

A nomad's life

Bactrian camels are the wandering nomads of central Asia, constantly moving between rocky mountains, stony deserts and sand dunes in search of food and water. After rain they may congregate near rivers or melting snows.

Today, although there are over two million domestic Bactrian camels, fewer than 1,000 of their wild relatives remain. Around 600 of these are spread across three separate sites in northwest China, with another 100 or so in the Gobi Desert in southwest Mongolia. The largest population lives in the Gashun Gobi Desert (Lop Nur) in Xinjiang Uighur Autonomous Region, China – used for 45 years as a nuclear weapons test site.

Spare tanks

Bactrian camels may travel vast distances each day in search of food and water, eating anything from shrubs and grass to thorns and saltbush. Although they can go long periods without drinking, they will consume up to 130 litres of water at a sitting to replenish body fluids. Their humps work like spare petrol tanks, storing fat reserves for times when food is scarce.

Herds usually number six to 20 related individuals led by a single adult male, though larger numbers may congregate around plentiful food or water. Breeding takes place in winter. Females have their first calf at around five years and can have one only every two years. Wild camels may live to around 40.

WHERE TO SEE IT

All areas where Bactrian camels remain are very remote. In China's Arjin Shan Nature Reserve (Southern Xinjiang) they are known to gather in Red-Blossom Tree Valley in spring. Annanba Nature Reserve, west of Dunhaung (Gansu Province) is more accessible and park staff may be able to assist. You can also find them in the Mongolian Gobi Desert, three weeks' drive from Ulan Bataar. Details at: www.cers.org.hk; www.wildcamels.com

THREATS

For centuries Bactrian camels have been hunted for their meat and skins. In more recent times massive habitat loss to illegal mining and industrial development has brought wild camels and domestic livestock into competition for food and water, leading to persecution from angry farmers. Scientists fear that the two forms will hybridise and eventually the distinct wild form will be lost.

8
EDGE RANK

Onager

Equus onager

Head/body length: 200–250cm
Height at shoulder: 100–140cm
Tail length: 30–50cm; **Weight:** 200–260kg

Iranian ass

The onager is the wild ass of the Middle East. It is larger than other Asian wild asses, with males being slightly bigger than females. Typical ass attributes include its pale sandy coat, dark stripe along the spine and white patches on the flanks, rump and belly. It also has a bristly black mane and a tuft at the tip of the tail. During cold winters, its coat grows thick and grey.

Home for this species is the flat semi-desert regions of Iran, where it roams widely but always within 30km of water. Once it was widespread throughout the central and southern plains, but today it is limited to just two protected areas: the Khar Touran National Park in Semnan Province and Bahram-e-Goor Reserve in Fars Province. About 470 animals are thought to survive at the former and another 100 or so at the latter, but perhaps only around 150 of these are breeding adults.

Speed merchant

Feeding is sparse in their barren desert home. Onagers browse on herbs, shrubs and trees and, like other horses, will also graze grasses when available. Most of their moisture comes from their food, though they do still visit water when possible – especially mothers that are suckling young.

The searing heat of the desert means that these creatures are more active at dawn and dusk when temperatures are cooler. If pressed they can gallop at speeds of up to 70km/h, which makes them the fastest of all wild horses.

Mares with foals live in small, temporary herds of around two to five. Dominant breeding stallions defend areas close to water and try and mate with any receptive females that come to drink. Mares produce a single foal after a gestation period of approximately a year. Foals remain with their mothers for the first two years.

WHERE TO SEE IT

Khar Touran National Park covers four million hectares and is Iran's second-largest reserve. Not only is it home to onager, but also dorcas gazelle, goitered gazelle, urial sheep and wild goat, all of which are vital prey for the last remaining population of Asiatic cheetahs. Daltours in Iran are members of Environment Protection Projects and can arrange trips. Details at: www.daltour.com; email: info@daltour.com

THREATS

Onagers are still poached for their meat, even in the protected areas that have become their last stronghold. Competition and overgrazing by domestic animals have reduced the availability of food and water. Disease and drought may also have a serious effect on the two small populations that remain.

14
EDGE RANK

Saiga antelope

Saiga tatarica

Head/body length: 125–145cm (male);
100–125cm (female); Height at shoulder: 60–80cm
Tail length: 6–12cm; Horn length: 20–25cm (males only)
Weight: 30–50kg (male); 20–45kg (female)

Nose job

This odd-looking animal resembles a cross between a gazelle and a sheep. Its most obvious feature is a bulbous nose, which looks like a prize-fighter's swollen conk. Its function is to warm up freezing inhaled air during the winter, filter out dust in the summer and help regulate blood temperature.

The coat is cinnamon-buff in colour, with a white belly and rump patch. In winter it becomes woolly and white, with a luxurious fringe on the chin and throat. Only males have horns, which are ridged at their base.

Taking steppes

The saiga lives in dry steppe grasslands and semi-arid deserts. It avoids broken or bushy terrain, preferring open areas where it can use its speed to escape predators.

Huge herds once swept across the steppes of central Asia in numbers that rivalled east Africa's wildebeest migration. Their range has since fragmented, with about 50,000 animals divided between one population in Russia (northwest Precaspian region) and three in Kazakhstan (the Ural, Ust'-Urt and Betpakdala). A much smaller separate population of about 1,500 survives in northwest Mongolia.

Baby boom

Saigas wander far and wide, grazing on grasses, herbs and shrubs, and migrate from steppe grasslands in summer to desert pastures in winter. During the December to January rut, males gather harems of females and defend them fiercely. Between fighting off rivals and keeping control of females they hardly have time to eat, and an amazing 90% may die.

Females synchronise birth so that an entire herd produces all its calves within one week in April. Twins are common. This glut of youngsters overwhelms predators. Calves are on their feet quickly and can travel within a few days, though they are not fully weaned until four months.

Both sexes mature very quickly: females can breed within a year, while males can mate at 20 months. This means that saiga populations can explode spectacularly if conditions are right, increasing by up to 60% a year. But turnover is high: though they may live to reach 10 to 12 years, few animals survive beyond four.

WHERE TO SEE IT

You can see saigas in two protected areas, the Chernye Zemli Biosphere Reserve in Kalmykia and the Stepnoi Sanctuary (Zakaznik) in Astrakhan Province. Access to the former is largely reserved for researchers, but the latter is setting up ecotourism as a source of funding. Details at: www.saiga-conservation.com

THREATS

Saiga have long been hunted for their horns, skin and meat. Intensive management during Soviet times kept populations relatively stable, but poaching increased with the collapse of the Soviet Union. Males were targeted for their horns, used in traditional oriental medicine. This severely skewed the sex ratio, causing breeding to fail and populations to plummet.

62
EDGE RANK

Japanese dormouse
Glirulus japonicus

Head/body length: 65–80mm
Tail length: 40–55mm
Weight: 15–40g

Little cutie
It's hard not to be entranced by this cute little ball of fluff, with its soft, olive-brown fur and big doe eyes. The long bushy tail and dark stripe down the back recall a tiny chipmunk, but in fact it belongs to a completely different family.

Unfortunately cuteness does not guarantee security. This rare rodent is found only on the Japanese islands of Honshu, Shikoku and Kyushu, where it inhabits mountain forests at elevations of 400–1,800m.

Sleeping beauty
Japanese dormice live in trees and are active at night, resting by day in round nests of lichen, twigs and bark. Since they also hibernate in winter, this means that they probably spend well over half their life asleep. In late summer, when food is plentiful, they fatten up to get ready for the long slumber. Their diet includes seeds, fruit, insects and birds' eggs. A litter of three to five babies is born in June or July, with sometimes a second litter in October.

WHERE TO SEE IT

China
Japan

Yatsugataka Highlands, two hours from Tokyo, is the most accessible site and has good hiking trails. Try spring or autumn, in early morning or at dusk. Yamane Nature Centre is a major dormouse research centre and has advice on accommodation and treks. Details at: www.keep.or.jp/english

THREATS
Loss of its mountain forest habitat is the main reason for this species' decline.

17 EDGE RANK

Slender loris
Loris tardigradus

Head/body length: 175–265mm; Weight: 100–350g

Boggle-eyes
This miniature, saucer-eyed primate appears to be wearing permanent jam-jar-bottom spectacles. It gets it name, though, from its exceptionally long, thin limbs. Its soft thick fur is grey to reddish-brown on top and whitish-grey below.

The slender loris is endemic to Sri Lanka, where it inhabits a variety of native forests. The lowland race (*L. t. tardigradus*) lives in the arid lowlands of the north and southeast, while the highland race (*L. t. nycticeboides*) frequents wet montane regions in the central highlands.

Group hug
Unlike most nocturnal primates, the slender loris enjoys company. Groups sleep huddled together by day in the treetops. After dark they head out separately in search of food.

This little creature shows great speed and agility in capturing insects, helped by the built-in night vision of its huge eyes. Other food includes gum, berries and bird's eggs.

WHERE TO SEE IT

India
Sri Lanka

Easiest to see in the dry scrub forests of the north, including at ruins such as Polonnaruwa Palace. Use an infrared light, as regular torches disrupt natural behaviour. The Loris Conservation Organisation offers good advice: www.loris-conservation.org/database/wild_survey/Survey

THREATS
Mainly habitat loss, including forest clearance for plantations and rice paddies. Pesticides also deplete insect prey. Other threats include roads and the traditional medicine trade.

22 EDGE RANK

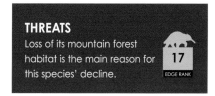

Giant panda

Ailuropoda melanoleuca

Head/body length: 120–50cm
Height at shoulder 70–80cm; Tail length: 12cm
Weight: 100–160kg (males 10% larger than females)

Veggie bear

The giant panda is perhaps the greatest icon of conservation today. Its unique combination of cuddly looks, distinctive markings, gentle demeanour and rarity has meant that from the moment of its discovery by French missionary Armand David in 1869, it has won the hearts of people the world over.

In fact, this roly-poly animal belongs to the bear family. It has the stout limbs and short tail of all its kind but, uniquely among bears, is a vegetarian, with a diet that consists almost entirely of bamboo. Especially wide molars and premolars, combined with powerful jaw muscles, help it to grind down this tough food. It also has a 'false thumb', formed from a modified wrist bone, to help hold it.

Mountain fugitive

This is a bear of temperate broadleaved and mixed coniferous forests. Though once seen in lowland ravines, it has been forced over time into the mountains. Historically it ranged right across eastern and southern China, even reaching northern Vietnam and Myanmar. Today it is restricted to six isolated mountain ranges in the provinces of Gansu, Shaanxi and Sichuan.

Accurate population figures are difficult to achieve. A major survey carried out in 2004 concluded that fewer than 1,600 pandas remained in the wild. However, recent genetic studies at Wanglang suggested this reserve had twice as many as previously thought.

Bamboo bonanza

Giant pandas can climb and swim, but spend most of their time on the ground looking for bamboo. This provides them with enough nutrition to survive – but only if they eat for up to 14 hours per day, consuming 12–38kg (up to 40% of their body weight). Since bamboo is evergreen, pandas can feed through the winter. Their diet sometimes extends to other plants and occasionally even meat.

Both males and females have home ranges, with those of males overlapping the ranges of two or more females. They keep in touch by calling and scent marking, but only get together for mating (March to May). The poor breeding performance of captive pandas has led to a popular misconception about their abilities to breed. But field research paints a different picture: a female on heat sometimes attracts the attentions of several males, who may even fight for her affections.

The single cub is born in the autumn. It is small, blind and helpless, and – at just 100–150g – a mere 0.001% of its mother's weight. The cub remains in a cave or hollow tree for the first month, while the mother carefully nurtures it. After weaning at eight to nine months it sticks with its mother until she conceives again 18 months later. Pandas reach sexual maturity at five to seven years and are thought to live for around 14–20 years in the wild.

WHERE TO SEE IT

The easiest place to see a giant panda in China is in Wolong Nature Reserve, Sichuan Province, at the China Conservation and Research Centre for Giant Pandas, where you can observe them in semi-captive conditions. Numerous wildlife tour operators organise trips. The more adventurous can search for pandas in the Qinling Mountains at both Foping and Laoxiancheng nature reserves. Sightings are infrequent, but specialist guides will show you how to track the animals. Who knows, you might get lucky. Details at: www.wildgiantpanda.com/reserve/laoxiancheng.htm; www.wildgiantpanda.com/reserve/foping.htm

THREATS

Habitat loss is the biggest threat. As forest is cleared for agriculture and timber, pandas are forced higher into the mountains. Illegal destruction even continues in reserves such as Wolong. Every few years bamboo flowers, seeds and then dies en masse, forcing pandas to look elsewhere as it recovers. With habitat now so fragmented, traditional migration routes have been cut off and pandas become stranded and risk starvation. Illegal poaching for pelts also continues, and pandas sometimes get caught in snares set for other animals.

18
EDGE RANK

Red panda
Ailurus fulgens

Head/body length: 510–635mm
Tail length: 280–485mm; Weight: 3–5kg

Raccoon relative

Unlike its giant namesake, the red panda is not a bear, but is actually related to raccoons – as you can tell from one glimpse of its distinctive facial markings and ringed tail. But it does share a peculiar bamboo-based lifestyle with its better-known, black-and-white cousin.

The thick fur is reddish-brown on top and black below, and is especially dense on its feet for warmth when it snows. The rounded white face has fluffy ears and reddish-brown markings, and the tail is boldly ringed in red and buff.

This species lives high (2,200–4,800m) in mist-shrouded, temperate forests with a dense bamboo understorey. It is restricted to the eastern Himalayas, including parts of Nepal, India, Bhutan and Myanmar, and isolated mountain ranges in western China (Sichuan, Yunnan and Tibet provinces).

Hollow treehouse

Red pandas like life in the trees, and have retractile claws and long tails to help them climb. Bamboo leaves are their favourite fare, although they may also snack on seeds, berries, roots and the occasional reptile or bird's egg. Like the giant panda they use a special wrist bone to help hold awkward bits of bamboo and, since bamboo is not very nutritious, must spend up to 13 hours a day feeding. They sleep periodically during the day in trees or fallen logs, and forage for food mostly at dawn and dusk.

Large male territories overlap with those of several female ones, but the two sexes rarely meet, except during the winter mating season. The following spring a female has one or two babies in a hollow tree nest. These are born blind and helpless, finally opening their eyes at 18 days. Because bamboo is such a poor diet, young pandas grow very slowly.

They stay in the nest for three months and stick close to their mothers until the next breeding season, taking a year to reach adult size and not reaching sexual maturity until about 18 months. Red pandas are thought to live for about eight to ten years in the wild.

WHERE TO SEE IT

Mongolia

China

In China your best bet is Yele Nature Reserve, 70km north of Mianning in Liangshan, Sichuan. Park staff can help you find pandas – you can sometimes even creep within 10m of one up a tree. At a breeding centre on the edge of the reserve you can see pandas roaming freely in a semi-wild enclosure. Singhalia National Park in Nepal has approachable wild red pandas, their population bolstered by the release of captive-bred animals from Darjeeling Zoo.

THREATS

The omnipresent spectre of habitat loss is the main threat: forests are cleared for timber, agriculture and livestock even within supposedly protected areas. Without bamboo to eat and trees to nest in red pandas can't survive. They are also hunted for their prized pelts, used to make traditional hats and clothing in China. Such hats are still regarded as good-luck marriage charms in Yunnan Province.

19
EDGE RANK

Wolverine

Gulo gulo

Head/body length: 65–95cm;
Tail length: 17–26cm; Weight: up to 25kg; average 15kg
(males), 10kg (females)

Giant weasel

Early scientists were unsure exactly which family
the wolverine belonged to. We now know that it is
the largest land-based member of the weasel family,
related to weasels, ferrets, badgers and otters. At first
glance it resembles a large, lumbering badger, with
its stocky body and short powerful legs. Its coat is
generally chocolate brown, with a pale stripe
around the rump and along the flanks, and its thick
fur and hairy paws help protect against freezing
winter conditions.

Wolverines are emblematic of northern wilderness,
where they inhabit large tracts of coniferous forest
and tundra. Their range extends across all northern
reaches of the globe, from the western United
States, Alaska and Canada, to Siberia, northern
Russia, northern Europe and Scandinavia. Before
human encroachment they roamed further south,
reaching California and the Baltic States in Europe.

Tough customer

This elusive beast has a reputation for power and
ferocity that belies its modest size, and its alternative
name of 'glutton' reflects its voracious appetite.
Powerful jaws and large teeth enable it to rip open
large carcasses and demolish frozen carrion and
bone. It takes a wide variety of prey and is easily
capable of downing animals as large as reindeer. It
will also scavenge from whale and seal carcasses, and
may drive larger predators from their kills. A carcass
that it can't polish off in one sitting is torn into
chunks and cached in various locations. Such food
may remain in cold storage for several months
before being consumed.

Unlike other carnivores, such as bears, wolverines
do not hibernate – even during the coldest winter.
Instead they rely on carrion, including carcasses of
domestic livestock, to see them through.

Little is known about the day-to-day lives of these
solitary animals. They may be active day or night,
and often sleep up trees. Home ranges can be vast,
depending on habitat and food availability. Males
and females associate only in the summer, for
mating, with births occurring the following spring
when thawing conditions make more food
available. Litters typically contain two or three
cubs, which are born blind and with white fur.

WHERE TO SEE IT

Kuhmo in Finland
is renowned as a
site for watching
wild wolverines. Lassi Rautianen has pioneered
wildlife photo safaris in the area and his trips offer
a good chance of seeing wolverines as well as
bears, wolves and moose. Trips run between April
and September and success is often dependent
on sitting and waiting in hides for long periods.
Details at: www.articmedia.fi/pageEnglish.html

THREATS

Being reliant on wilderness areas and
sensitive to disturbance, the wolverine's
decline has mirrored the advance of
humanity. Historically it has been hunted
for its fur and persecuted as a predator
of domestic reindeer and other
livestock – although in reality
such predation is minimal.

354
EDGE RANK

Amami rabbit
Pentalagus furnessi

Head/body length: 430–510mm
Ear length: 45cm
Tail length: 15mm
Weight: up to 2kg

Relic rabbit

This puzzling bunny is a 'living fossil', descended from ancestors that roamed Asia 10–20 million years ago. Its small eyes, short ears and short limbs clearly set it apart from common rabbits. It also has unusually woolly fur and long claws.

Confined to the islands of Amami, Oshima and Tokunoshima in Japan's Ryukyu Archipelago, this species inhabits old-growth forest and can also tolerate disturbed forest edges. It forages at night for various plants, especially Japanese pampas grass in summer and acorns in winter. Only 3,000–5,000 survive, mostly on Amami.

A female gives birth twice a year to two or three young. She seals them in their den, returning at night to dig away the blockage and allow them to suckle, before resealing the hole with the loose soil.

WHERE TO SEE IT

Amami Gunto Quasi National Park on Amami Oshima is the best place, reached by air from Kyushu. Amami Park, a cultural and wildlife centre, is adjacent to the airport and will advise on night walks. Details at: www.amamipark.com/en_index

THREATS

Early threats came from hunting. In 1921 the rabbit was given full legal protection. Today's threats include predation by dogs, cats and introduced mongooses, as well as massive habitat loss.

=43
EDGE RANK

Steppe pika
Ochotona pusilla

Head/body length: about 15cm
Weight: about 175–200g

Rabbit relative

Pikas (sometimes called mouse hares) are small relatives of rabbits and hares, with short round ears and barely visible tails. This species is dark greyish-brown above with a paler belly.

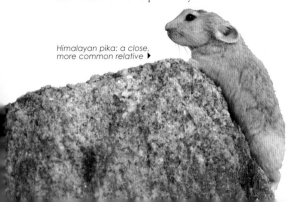

Himalayan pika: a close, more common relative ▶

Haymaker

Pikas range across the mountainous regions of North America, and central and eastern Asia. This species inhabits meadows and steppes from the Ural Mountains east across southern Russia and northern Kazakhstan.

For such a little animal the steppe pika has a big voice, its short, high-pitched call being audible from some distance. It is primarily nocturnal – unlike most pikas – and digs burrows to rest in during the day. But it cannot tolerate warm weather and does not hibernate in winter. Females have three to five litters a year with an average of eight young each – exceptionally up to 13.

Grasses, leaves and flower stalks are the steppe pika's main diet. It harvests food during late summer and early autumn to store for winter. These food stores look like little piles of hay.

WHERE TO SEE IT

Orenburgskiy Nature Reserve in the South Urals, Russia, is perhaps the best site. Look out for their burrows and listen for their calls. Details at: www.welcome-ural-ru/tours

THREATS

The limited range of this species makes it especially vulnerable to habitat loss from agriculture and grazing stock. Its intolerance of higher temperatures may also leave it susceptible to global warming.

120
EDGE RANK

Sloth bear

Melursus ursinus

Head/body length: 140–190cm
Height at shoulder: 60–90cm
Weight: 80–145kg (males); 55–95kg (females)

Barely typical

This animal is the celebrated Baloo from Kipling's *Jungle Book*. But it is hardly your typical bear, being a smallish and mostly nocturnal insect eater. Early explorers coined the name, having seen it lying upside down in trees like a sloth.

The black coat is surprisingly shaggy – especially given the hot climate where it lives – and sports a distinctive creamy 'necklace' marking on the chest. The long pale muzzle ends in large protrusible lips, which are adaptations for an insect-based diet, as is its lack of upper incisors. The immensely strong forelegs are equipped with long curved claws, used to dig open concrete-hard termite mounds and break into tree holes to get to bees' nests.

Sloth bears occur in a variety of habitats, from grasslands and thorn scrub to deciduous and evergreen forest. They are found in many parts of the Indian subcontinent, including India, Nepal, Bhutan, Bangladesh and Sri Lanka.

Honey fiend

The scientific name of this bear, *Melursus*, reflects its insatiable craving for honey. It readily climbs trees to raid bees' nests, paying little attention to the stings of the angry owners. Other food includes ants and termites, which it sucks in through a gap in its front teeth, and a variety of fruits and berries in season.

This is a solitary and largely nocturnal species, except for mothers with their cubs, and marks its territory by stripping bark from trees. Females give birth to an average of two cubs, which they often conceal in the base of a hollow tree. After three months these emerge and ride on on her back like little jockeys – a habit that is unique among bears. Cubs stay with their mother for up to 2.5 years.

WHERE TO SEE IT

You can see sloth bears in many well-known parks and reserves on the subcontinent, including Ranthambhore, Bandhavgarh, Kanha, Pench, Bandipur, Nagarhole, Mudumalai and Melghat in India, Royal Chitwan and Bardia in Nepal, and Yala in Sri Lanka. Sightings are unpredictable, though more frequent in April and May when the bears feed on fallen mohwa flowers (*Madhuca latifolia*). Chances are much better at Daroji Sloth Bear Sanctuary, 15km from Hampi in North Karnataka, which is home to over 120 bears. Details at: www.karnataka.com/slothbear

THREATS

Although sloth bears remain widespread, their numbers have fallen dramatically. For centuries they have been poached for their gall bladders and other body parts, prized in traditional oriental medicine. They were also the original 'dancing bears' – traditionally trained by the Qalandars people, who would abduct a cub, remove its teeth and claws, and put a metal ring and rope through its nose to keep it under control. Thankfully, this barbaric practice has now been outlawed, and many ex-performing bears have been relocated to semi-wild sanctuaries.

339
EDGE RANK

Eurasia

Martin Walters

It is hard now to imagine the wildlife of Eurasia in its most natural state, so radical has been the impact of people and their activities. Yet near-natural habitats do persist: the brooding coniferous forests of Siberia still swathe huge tracts of northern Russia and the barren high peaks of the Himalayan mountains retain much of their original character, as do the parched deserts of central Asia and Mongolia. In Europe and much of lowland Asia, however, the influence of people on the wildlife is inescapable. Centuries of forest clearance and wetland drainage have transformed the original habitats, modifying or replacing them with agriculture, industry and urbanisation.

The region's topography has been shaped by a long alternating history of glaciation and recolonisation. About two million years ago huge sheets of ice covered much of Europe and Asia for long periods, wiping out vegetation and pushing the wildlife southwards. Since about 14,000 years ago, however, the ice has been gradually receding, a process that is now accelerated by human-induced global warming. With the ice in retreat, people began to spread across the region – slowly at first, but then at an ever-increasing pace. Their advance brought fundamental and long-lasting effects on the natural world.

Before people, the wildlife had been quite different, with large mammals such as mammoths wandering the cool plains of northern Europe. As recently as 700,000 years ago animals such as hippos, rhinos, elephants and sabre-toothed cats roamed the region. Recent finds have proved that there were people living in Britain at this time, having crossed from mainland Europe by a land bridge that no longer exists, and in southern Europe as early as 800,000 years ago. But these scattered groups would then have had little overall effect on the 'untamed' nature around them.

Beasts of burden

The domestication of animals first took place in Eurasia and may have begun as early as 10,000BC. Remains of domestic sheep have been dated to about 9,000BC in the Middle East. Dogs were domesticated from wolves and evolved under human selection into the multitude of forms we know today. Sheep and goats were bred to provide people with wool, meat and milk, cattle for milk and leather, and horses for traction and transport. These domesticated species were a major factor in allowing our own to harness the natural world to its own ends.

In time, however, agriculture spread northwards across Europe, reaching central Europe from further south around 4,500BC along the river valleys of the Danube and Rhine. This process had started even earlier in Asia, India and China. As people began to plant crops, fell forests and hunt animals for food, so their impact on the species around them increased. By about 3,000BC people had spread across most of Europe and the forests were already shrinking, plundered for timber and to make way for farming.

▲ Mammoths were among many prehistoric mammals to feel the impact of human migration.

Greek amphora from 600BC depicting Heracles capturing Cerberus, the many-headed hound ▶

The Eurasian region is the home of the science of natural history as we know it today. The Greek philosopher Aristotle (384–322BC) was among the earliest Europeans whose observations of the natural world have survived, including his ground-breaking *Historia Animalium* (On the History of Animals). However, natural history really took off as a formal science in the 18th century. Carl Linnaeus (1707–78) was a major figure in what became known as the Golden Age of Botany, when European scientists first began travelling to collect a huge range of species. The Linnaean system of naming and classifying animals and plants laid the foundations on which naturalists were able to build their collections and make sense of the diversity of the natural world.

▲ *Carl Linnaeus (1707–78). Swedish botanist and founder of taxonomy*

▲ *Giant panda, drawn in 1927 by Friedrich Wilhelm Kuhnert, 58 years after the animal was discovered*

Background: Cave painting from 12,000 BC in Altamira Caves, Spain, depicting hunted animals

Eastern horizons

Marco Polo (1254–1324) set out from Venice aged 17 on a 9,000km, three-and-a-half-year journey that had a huge influence on Western knowledge of Asia. He followed the ancient trade route known as the Silk Road and in 1275 reached the residence of the Mongol Emperor Kublai Khan in what is now Beijing. From here he made missions across China, Burma and India, probably the first time these places had been seen by Western eyes. Many centuries later evangelism opened a new avenue of zoological exploration. The French missionary Père Armand David (1826–1900) visited Mongolia and China in the 1860s and collected material for natural history museums in France. Among more than 60 mammals that were then unknown to science, he discovered the giant panda and the deer species now known in his honour as Père David's deer.

Other explorer-naturalists of note included George Forrest (1873–1932), a Scot who discovered over 1,200 plants new to science, and Robert Swinhoe, who amassed an impressive collection of new birds in China and Taiwan. The Russian zoologist Przevalski, in whose honour the now-extinct horse was named, conducted his expeditions on a grand scale, habitually covering over 7,000km. Meanwhile exploration also originated from further east: by as early as 1709 the Japanese author Atsunobu Kaibara had published a 21-volume work (*Yamato Honzo*), of which the 15th volume was dedicated to birds and covered 99 species.

Medallion depicting Marco Polo (1254–1324) ▲

Martin Walters *is a writer and naturalist, based in Cambridge, with a particular interest in the natural history of China and its culture. His latest publications include a guide to the wildlife of China.*

Indian rhinoceros

Rhinoceros unicornis

Head/body length: 310–380cm
Height at shoulder: 148–186cm
Tail length: 70–80cm; Horn length: up to 60cm
**Weight: average 1,800kg; up to 2,700kg (male),
1,600kg (female)**

Armour plating

Unmistakable: an armour-clad giant, with a
backside that looks like steel plate covered in rivets.
This is the largest of the Asian rhinos and the
continent's second-largest land animal.

The Indian rhino has a virtually hairless, pewter-
grey hide, although the precise colour depends on
where it's been wallowing. Unlike the two African
rhinos, it has just one horn. It also has a semi-
prehensile upper lip to help grasp food.

Swamp monster

This rhino likes it wet. It lives on alluvial
floodplains, favouring areas with tall grasses or
reeds, plus swampy areas (*jheels*) and adjacent forests.
Individuals may move around seasonally, especially
to higher ground during the monsoon floods.

Historically Indian rhinos occupied a swathe of
territory known as the *Terai*, effectively comprising
the floodplains of the great Ganges, Bhramaputra
and Indus rivers. Today this habitat is massively
reduced, with the rhinos now confined to pockets
in southwest Nepal and northeast India. Current
estimates suggest a total of no more than 2,500
rhinos, with some 65% of these being found in
Kaziranga National Park in Assam.

Dung roaming

The diet is mainly grass, though it also includes
some leaves and twigs – for which the prehensile
upper lip comes in useful. This diet needs regular
mineral supplements, so the rhinos visit favourite
salt licks regularly. Feeding takes place mostly
during early mornings and evenings. In the heat of
the day they flop down neck-deep in water or a
mud wallow to keep cool.

These solitary creatures aim generally to avoid one
another, though small groups sometimes gather at
wallows. Dominant males can be very aggressive,
engaging intruders in fights that sometimes prove

fatal, and inflicting deep wounds not with their horn, but with the tusk-like lower teeth. Otherwise Indian rhinos are shy and will generally retreat from danger, although mothers will stick around to defend calves. Their acute hearing and sense of smell make up for their poor eyesight.

The toilet habits of these creatures are remarkably fastidious. Several animals defecate on a dung heap, or midden, which can reach 1m high and 5m wide. This acts as a communication point: each rhino scrapes its hind feet through the pile then spreads its scent as it wanders along its regular trails (or 'dandies').

Females become sexually mature at five to seven years and usually give birth to a single calf every three to four years. Calves drink 20–30 litres of their mother's milk per day, adding easily 2kg in weight. Tigers may occasionally take calves, but adults have no predators other than people and may live 30–45 years in the wild.

WHERE TO SEE IT

By far the best place to see this wonderful animal is Kaziranga National Park in Assam, northeast India, where a magical early morning elephant ride into the marshes gets you up close and personal with rhinos. Jeep safaris here are also very good, and numerous rhinos may be visible from strategic watchtowers. A similar experience is possible in Nepal's Chitwan and Bardia national parks, although the rhinos here are less numerous and probably more timid due to recent poaching.

THREATS

The decline of this species started with the draining of marshes and expansion of agricultural land. Hunting for sport and pest control (when rhinos raided crops) also took its toll. By the beginning of the 20th century, the Indian rhino was already considered to be a 'vanishing species'. More recently, the main threat has come from poachers, who supply the illegal trade in horns and other body parts used in traditional Asian medicine. With rhino horn reaching US$20,000–30,000 per kilo in certain east Asian markets, poaching has become ever more sophisticated, often outwitting the high-level protection that the species now receives.

74
EDGE RANK

Snow leopard

Panthera (Uncia) uncia

Head/body length: 100–130cm
Height at shoulder: 55–60cm
Tail length: 80–100cm
Weight: 45–55kg (males); 35–40kg (females)

WHERE TO SEE IT

Seeing a wild snow leopard, once mere fantasy, is now a real – though very challenging – possibility. In Hemis National Park in Ladakh, India, tour companies run snow leopard treks in March and November. Alternatively try Chitral Gol National Park in northwestern Pakistan in December or February/March. Details at: www.discoveryinitiatives.co.uk/ discover/trip/India/Snow_Leopard_trek; www.snowleopardconservancy.org

THREATS

Snow leopards have paid the price for their exquisite fur coat. For centuries they were hunted mercilessly, especially to supply the fickle fashion houses of the West. Thankfully attitudes have now changed. Nonetheless, snow leopard pelts and body parts are still in demand for tribal costumes and oriental medicine markets. In places where the snow leopard's natural prey has been hunted out, hungry cats turn to domestic stock and so suffer retaliation from angry farmers.

326
EDGE RANK

Cool cat

The almost mythical snow leopard is undisputed top cat of the mountains. This beautiful animal has a smoky, yellowish-grey coat patterned with dark, smudgy rosettes and spots. Its luxuriant fur helps it withstand extreme cold, and its thick tail makes a perfect scarf to wrap around the body and face.

Other special survival adaptations include large lungs to make the most of scant oxygen at high altitude and large paws that act like snow shoes. Short legs and a long tail also help it to balance when leaping around the rocky hillsides.

High plains drifter

This feline mountaineer inhabits the remote high regions of central Asia, generally at 1,800–5,500m, where it can survive winter temperatures of −40°C. It may also venture down into areas of scrub, steppe and open forest, even as low as 900m in the Gobi Desert. The 3,500–6,000 snow leopards that remain are scattered from the western Himalayas to the southern Mongolia steppes, with the healthiest population being in the Tibetan region of China.

Loner's life

Snow leopards are the ultimate loners, ghosting through the ridges and valleys like wisps of smoke. Their home ranges are 30–65km² in areas of plentiful prey, but much larger elsewhere. Males and females get together only during the January–March mating season, making unearthly cries that may explain some tales of yetis. Females give birth to two to three cubs in a rocky den, usually in late spring or early summer. The youngsters become independent after two years.

These secretive cats hunt at dawn and dusk, stalking to within 30–40m of their victim before a final deadly dash. Wild goats and sheep, such as blue sheep and ibex, are favourite prey, while the odd marmot or hare makes a tasty snack in summer.

Long-eared jerboa

Euchoreutes naso

Head/body length: 70–90mm
Hind foot length: 40–46mm; **Tail length:** 150–162mm
Weight: 24–38g

Jack-in-a-box

This bouncing jack-in-a-box of a rodent is about the size of a large mouse, with outrageous ears that appear to have been borrowed from a rabbit. It also has enormous back legs to power its leaps, and a long, white-tufted tail that acts as a prop when standing upright. Its fur is reddish-yellow to pale russet, with white underparts.

Desert dweller

The long-eared jerboa lives in sandy deserts with low shrub cover. It ranges from western Xinjiang in northwest China to southern Mongolia, where it has been recorded at ten sites in the Trans Altai Govi Desert and Alashan Plateau.

Scientists know very little about this creature. They assume that, like other jerboas, it is nocturnal and spends the day in burrows. Unlike its cousins, however, it seems to prefer insects to seeds.

WHERE TO SEE IT
Try the Taklamakan Desert region in Xinjiang Province – at Hami to the east of Xinjiang and Minfeng in the south. Locals will help you look. Check for tracks in the dunes and then return after dark. Spring and autumn are best, just after dusk and just before dawn.

THREATS
The biggest worry concerns the growing population of people and their increasing numbers of livestock, which severely degrade the jerboa's habitat.

81
EDGE RANK

Takin

Budorcas taxicolor

Head/body length: 170–220cm
Height at shoulder: 100–130cm; **Horn length:** up to 60cm
Weight: up to 350kg (males); up to 250kg (females)

Shaggy goat stories

The takin looks like a cross between a billy goat and a shaggy cow, and belongs to a group of animals called goat antelopes. It has a distinctive Roman nose, and horns in both sexes. The shaggy coat is generally a pale fawn, though in one race, the golden takin, it is lustrous orange-yellow – which may explain the 'golden fleece' of ancient Greek legend.

Bamboo stinker

Takin inhabit forested valleys and bamboo forests at 1,000–4,500m. Small family groups wander the eastern Himalayas, ranging from India into western China. They nibble a variety of leaves, buds and grasses, and also visit mineral deposits for salt. During summer grazing herds 300-strong gather on the high slopes. They split up and retreat to lower forests during winter. A single calf is born in March–April.

Unlike most animals, which have specific scent glands, the takin produces a pungent secretion over its whole body. It also has a distinctive alarm call, which sounds a bit like a smoker's cough.

WHERE TO SEE IT
A serious challenge. Changqing Nature Reserve in Shaanxi Province, China, offers a chance: in winter takin descend to lower slopes, where expert park guides track them. Foping Nature Reserve, also in Shaanxi, and Tangjiahe Nature Reserve in Sichuan, are also possible sites. Details at: www.cqpanda.com; www.wildgiantpanda.com/reserve/foping.htm

THREATS
The inaccessibility of their habitat means we know very little about takin populations and distribution. But habitat loss and disease certainly pose a threat.

455
EDGE RANK

Ganges river dolphin

Platanista gangetica

Body length: 150–250cm
Weight: up to 150kg (females larger than males)

Deep and murky

This species looks very similar to the Yangzte river dolphin (see opposite), with its stocky body, long beak and large visible teeth. Its dorsal fin is a low triangular hump and its dark grey-brown body may sometimes be light pinkish below. With no lenses in its eyes it is effectively blind, able to perceive only light and dark.

The Ganges river dolphin frequents murky rivers, but may sometimes be found in clearer waters. It prefers deep, slow-flowing stretches where prey congregates. Once it occurred throughout the great Ganges-Brahmaputra river system of India, Bangladesh and Nepal (and possibly Bhutan).

WHERE TO SEE IT

In India this species is perhaps most easily seen in the National Chambal Sanctuary, on the Chambal River, south of Agra. Chambal Safari Lodge runs dedicated boat trips. It may also be seen in deep pools on the Karnali River in Bardia National Park, west Nepal. In southern Bangladesh it appears to be relatively common in the lower Sangu River and there are plans to establish a sanctuary here. The Vikramshila Gangetic Dolphin Sanctuary in Bihar, India, is the only designated protected area for this dolphin, but it currently has no formal conservation plan and illegal activities continue. Details at: www.wdcs.org; www.chambalsafari.com

THREATS

The primary threat is the damming of rivers for irrigation and electricity generation. This reduces flows, affects prey species, isolates dolphin populations and prevents their seasonal migrations. More than 40 barrages and high dams have been constructed in the Ganges-Brahmaputra-Megna and Karnaphuli-Sangu river systems in the past half-century. Pollution from industrial and domestic effluents, hunting for meat or oil, and accidental entanglement in fishing nets also take their toll.

=65
EDGE RANK

Today, however, it is restricted to the Ganges-Brahmaputra-Meghna and Karnaphuli-Sangu river systems in Bangladesh and India, with a few individuals surviving in the Karnali River of west Nepal. No more than 1,200–2,000 remain.

Scraping the bottom

These dolphins generally live alone, but pods of five or more have been seen where feeding is good. They feed by swimming on their side, trailing a flipper in the mud along the bottom and then using their beaks to snap up any small fish and invertebrates that they disturb. Like bats, they also use echolocation to find their way around and locate food – emitting a stream of noises then orientating themselves by the returning echoes from objects around them.

During the dry season the dolphins remain in deep pools or channels, migrating upstream to tributaries after the monsoon. A single calf is born every two years. It reaches sexual maturity at around ten years and may live to around 30.

Baiji (Yangtze river dolphin)

Lipotes vexillifer

Length: 140–215cm (male); 185–250cm (female)
Weight: 42–125kg (male); 65–165 kg (female)

WHERE TO SEE IT

Mongolia

China

Here's an opportunity to make a name for yourself. Realistically, your chances of seeing the baiji are negligible. However for a species to be officially classified as extinct it has to pass one generation without a sighting, so this leaves room for a glimmer of hope. If any individual is found, conservationists plan to translocate it to Tian-e-Zhou (Swan) oxbow lake near Shishou City, a semi-natural reserve.
Details at: http://baiji.org/in-depth/baiji.html

THREATS

The baiji has long been regarded as the world's most endangered cetacean. With over 400 million people living within the Yangtze River catchments, its home has been desecrated by pollution, transportation, fishing, abstraction and industrial development. Countless dolphins have been killed by accidental trapping in gill nets and other forms of fishing, while many have also died in boat collisions.

1
EDGE RANK

Going, going, gone

It's an unflattering description for such a graceful creature, but the baiji looks like a giant blue-grey sausage with a fin and a beak. This beak is longer and more upturned than in other freshwater dolphins. It has little use for eyesight, having evolved for life in murky waters, so its eyes are tiny and barely functional. Females are generally larger than males.

This freshwater species is endemic to the Yangtze River Basin in eastern China, where it was once a common sight at the confluences of the main

PROBABLY EXTINCT

Yangtze channel and smaller side streams and rivers. Historically it ranged from the river mouth upstream to 50km above Gezhouba Dam. But no sighting in the past 30 years has been more than 135km upstream of the river mouth.

Its decline has been precipitous: in 1997 surveys found just 17 individuals, one year later this was down to seven, and by 1999 to just four.

Unconfirmed sightings by local fishermen offered a flicker of hope. However, the latest survey (early 2007) failed to find a single dolphin in 3,500km between the city of Wuhan and the Yangtze Delta. There is a real possibility the species is now extinct.

Not a splash

Baiji once lived in small pods, with up to 16 individuals gathering where prey was plentiful. The few more recent sightings have generally been of pairs or solitary dolphins. They feed during darkness and early morning, taking a wide range of freshwater fish, and have a characteristic habit of breaking the surface smoothly without a splash.

Evidence suggests baiji may once have travelled far up and down stream, driven by seasonal changes in water level. Females reach maturity at eight years and give birth to one young approximately every two years. One captive male, 'Qi-Qi', survived in the Wuhan dolphinarium for over 22 years.

Tiger

Panthera tigris

Head/body length: 2.5–3.2m (male); 2–2.65m (female)
Height at shoulder: 80–110cm
Tail length: 80–100cm
Weight: 180–380kg (male); 100–200kg (female)

Star in stripes

Everyone's favourite animal? The biggest of the big cats, the tiger occupies an exclusive place in the human psyche. Today its irresistible blend of beauty, grace, power and mystery is used to sell everything from breakfast cereals to petrol. Yet, amazingly, this magnificent creature might be the first big cat we condemn to extinction.

Tigers vary considerably. Males are substantially larger than females, and Siberian tigers (the largest subspecies) are almost double the weight of Sumatran tigers (the smallest). Colour ranges from a deep reddish-orange (Sumatran) to a pale yellow-ochre (Siberian). Each individual has a unique pattern of stripes – like fingerprints.

Burning bright – but only just

Wild tigers need three main things: enough prey, fresh water and dense cover in which to hide. Suitable habitat varies widely across the species' range, from tropical rainforests to tall grasslands, mangroves, dry woodland and coniferous forest with thick winter snow.

Their range once spanned much of eastern, central and southern Asia. But four races – the Bali tiger, Javan tiger, Caspian tiger and, probably, the south China tiger – have already been driven to extinction. Today five remain: the Bengal tiger, in India, Bangladesh, Nepal and Bhutan; the Indochinese tiger, in Cambodia, China, Myanmar, Thailand and Vietnam; the Malayan tiger, in southern Malaysia; the Sumatran tiger, restricted to Sumatra; and the Siberian tiger, confined to far eastern Russia.

At the turn of the 20th century there were probably more than 100,000 wild tigers. Today there are at best 3,000. The most 'numerous' race is the Bengal tiger, of which around 1,200–1,500 are scattered around the Indian subcontinent.

WHERE TO SEE IT

Wild tigers are not
hard to see in one of
India's famous
reserves, such as
Bandhavgarh or
Kanha. However, sightings generally involve
the same handful of individuals. In Nepal,
Royal Chitwan and Bardia are also good,
though less reliable. Numerous tour operators
offer trips, with peak time being November–
April. Elsewhere your chances are very slim.
For a real challenge, try tracking Siberian
tigers: contact the Phoenix Fund in
Vladivostok email: phoenix@mail.primorye.ru
or Dalintourist Vladivostok email: zox@dalin
tourist.ru, or visit www.wildlifeextra.com/
udege_national-park.html

THREATS
The tiger's massive decline started
during the last century with merciless
trophy hunting, which finally became
illegal in India in 1969. Rapid human
population growth and increasing
deforestation made things worse. For
the past 30 years poaching for the
illegal fur trade and oriental medicine
markets has increased, and the demand
for tiger parts is rising with increased
affluence in Asia. An exploding human
population has hunted out much of
the tiger's natural prey, forcing
tigers to turn on domestic
livestock and thus run into
conflict with farmers.

=331
EDGE RANK

The largest single population is that of the Siberian
tiger, with 450–480 animals.

Surprisingly sociable
Tigers generally tread a solitary path, but can be
sociable at times. Males and females each defend
separate territories against intruders of the same
sex, marking boundaries by scratching trees,
spraying with urine and leaving scats (droppings).
A male's home patch is larger and will overlap with
up to four or more female territories.

A male's job is to provide a secure environment in
which females can raise his cubs. He visits each of
the females whose territories overlap his own, and
can be surprisingly tender towards his offspring.
Litters of two to four cubs are born deep in the
mother's territory. They learn to hunt from around
six months, but remain dependent on their mother
for up to 20 months.

Tigers use cover and supreme camouflage to stalk
their prey. They usually hunt after dark, but
occasionally grab a meal by day. Typical prey
comprises deer, wild pigs and wild cattle, though
may include smaller animals like monkeys. After a
large meal a tiger must drink. Unlike most cats, it
will often enter streams and lakes to cool off.

Conserving wildlife in Eurasia

The vast landmass of Eurasia embraces dozens of different ecoregions, from the Siberian tundra to the Mediterranean basin, via boreal forest, steppe, mountain and desert. In western Europe it contains eight of the ten wealthiest countries in the world, yet parts of central Asia are war-torn and impoverished. Unsurprisingly the conservation issues facing the region reflect these wide disparities.

Hunting the hunters

The persecution of predators has a long and depressing history across Eurasia. The trio of grey wolf, Eurasian lynx and brown bear are, ecologically speaking, the top predators across much of the northern part of the region, but in many European countries they have been eradicated completely or exist in barely tenable numbers. National policy and attitudes now dictate their fortunes: for example, Norway and Sweden share a small wolf population, but while Sweden advocates strict protection, Norway recently authorised a cull. Conservation initiatives are afoot, however, and wolves are among several species now receiving support from the Large Carnivore Initiative for Europe (*www.lcie.org*) via a variety of projects.

But persecution isn't the only hazard that predators face. Habitat loss and fragmentation, along with a sustained assault upon the numbers of its key prey species, the rabbit, has reduced the wild population of the Iberian lynx to little more than 100. The World Wildlife Fund (*www.wwf.org.uk*) is supporting a two-pronged attack to save this species: not only must its habitat be protected and expanded, but a captive-breeding programme to produce animals for eventual reintroduction and to preserve maximum genetic diversity is crucial. WWF is also calling for measures that will reduce lynx road deaths.

▲ **Options open:** *The steppe-lands of central Europe and Asia hold rich but fragile ecosystems.*

Taking steppes

The steppe region of Eurasia stretches from Hungary to the eastern edge of Mongolia, forming a link between the forested regions of the north and the desert or coastal areas further south. It is home to such endangered species as Saiga antelope and steppe pika, but vast tracts have been converted to agriculture – much of it so intensive that little space is left for native wildlife. Among the few intact remaining fragments is the Khomutovski Steppe Nature Reserve (www.cybertruffle.org.uk/khomstep/index.htm) in the Ukraine. Land managers here are applying principles of open-country conservation through liaison with managers of wildlife-rich Ministry of Defence land in the UK.

▲ **Road works:** *Underpasses like this help Iberian lynxes get around safely.*

Forests under fire

One of the key Eurasian biomes is the belt of coniferous forest that extends from northern Scotland across Scandinavia and all the way to the far east of Russia. These boreal forests, also known as taiga, have a crucial global role as carbon sinks, and their loss and the associated release of carbon into the atmosphere

Mountain marvels

Mountainous regions don't lend themselves to development or agriculture, but even 6,000m high in Nepal and Tibet snow leopards do not escape the attentions of hunters. These stunning cats are so rare and elusive that they are seldom observed – even by dedicated scientific expeditions – but their pelts and body parts

The forested mountains of western and central China support a diversity of rare endemic animals, including the takin, the golden snub-nosed monkey, the white-lipped deer and the giant panda. The Sichuan Giant Panda Sanctuaries, home to more than 30% of the world's giant pandas, covers 924,500ha and comprises seven nature reserves and nine scenic

contributes to global warming. Logging for timber, and to clear land for oil and gas extraction costs Siberia more than three million hectares of forest a year. Species dependent on this habitat include the endangered Siberian tiger and Siberian musk deer. Taiga Rescue Network (*www.taigarescue.org*) works to strengthen the co-operation between individuals, NGOs and indigenous peoples to protect and restore boreal forests, and harvest them sustainably. The Forest Stewardship Council (*www.fscus.org*) certifies companies that use wood from sustainably managed forest: 92 Russian companies currently hold FSC certificates.

command so high a price on the black market that hunters will go to great lengths to track them down. The Snow Leopard Trust (*www.snowleopard.org*) has been working to conserve snow leopards and their habitat since 1981. In 2006 it collaborated on a project to fit a snow leopard with a GPS collar, which has yielded invaluable insights into this species' way of life. Biosphere Expeditions (*www.biosphere-expeditions.org*) offers volunteers the chance to join researchers in the Altai mountains.

▲ **Pine away:** *Northern Eurasia's extensive boreal forests are fast vanishing under the loggers' saws.*
▲ **Track suit:** *This snow leopard has been fitted with a GPS collar, for researchers to track her movements.*
▲ **Little and large:** *Reluctant to mate and slow to mature, giant pandas are notoriously difficult to breed in captivity.*

parks in the Qionglai and Jiajin mountains. One of the reserves is the Wolong National Nature Reserve (*www.pandaclub.net*), which harbours 300 wild pandas. It also has a successful captive breeding programme for the species, with a view to carrying out reintroductions of young pandas into suitable areas of habitat.

Eurasia's conservation challenges are legion, but if flagship animals like the giant panda and Siberian tiger can be saved from extinction, this is sure to fuel hope and determination in addressing the many other species whose future hangs in the balance.

Southeast Asia

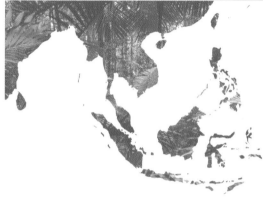

Bound by China to the north, the Indian subcontinent to the west and Australasia to the east and south, the Southeast Asian region comprises a small but distinct part of the Asian landmass. It also encompasses a seemingly innumerable collection of islands, both large and small, many of which form part of Indonesia, the world's largest archipelago.

The region, and especially its array of islands, is biologically amongst the richest and most complex on earth. It is home to iconic species such as orang-utans, elephants, tigers and rhinos whose lineage stems from the Asian continent, but also supports species, including a number of marsupials, that have affinities with Australasia. This is a consequence of the region lying at the convergence of two great tectonic plates, which has effectively brought once far-separated groups of species into their present-day intimate juxtaposition – a phenomenon first explained by the eminent Victorian naturalist Alfred Russel Wallace (see page 49).

Southeast Asia has a predominantly equatorial climate and supports the world's third largest rainforest, after the Amazon and Congo. However, there is plenty of variation, particularly where mountains occur. At 4,095m, Mount Kinabalu on Borneo is the highest point between the Himalayas and Puncak Jaya in Western New Guinea (formerly Irian Jaya), and rises like a citadel from the surrounding lowlands. It is effectively a highland 'island' and so supports an extraordinary diversity of unusual endemic species.

◀ *The function of a male proboscis monkey's bulbous nose is uncertain. It may be that females are more attracted to the males with big noses.*

Pygmy hog
p54
Assam, India
(Manas National
Park and Barnadi
Wildlife Sanctuary)

Bumblebee bat
p47
Western Thailand
(Sai Yok National
Park); southeast
Myanmar

Pygmy slow loris
p55
Vietnam and Laos
to southern China
and Cambodia

Black gibbon
p51
Laos, Vietnam and
China (Yunnun
Province)

**Palawan stink
badger**
p47
Islands of Palawan
and Busuanga
(Philippines)

Visayan warty pig
p55
Islands of Negros
and western
mountains of
Panay (Philippines)

Hoolock gibbon
p43
From Northeast India
and Bangladesh to
Myanmar and
southwest China

Dinagat moonrat
p42
Islands of Dinagat,
Siargao and
Bucas Grande,
Philippines

Asian elephant
p44
India, Sri Lanka and
Nepal to Vietnam and
Malaysia; also Sumatra
and northern Borneo

Proboscis monkey
p46
Coatal Borneo
(Sabah, Sarawak
and Kalimantan)

Orang-utan
p52
Sumatra species:
northern Sumatra
(Indonesia); Borneo
species: Kalimantan,
Sarawak and Sabah
(Borneo)

Bornean bay cat
p50
Central Borneo

Sumatran rabbit
p42
Barisan Mountains,
west and
southwest Sumatra
(Indonesia)

Sumatran rhinoceros
p40
Sumatra (Indonesia);
Peninsular Malaysia;
Sabah (Borneo)

Javan rhinoceros
p41
Java (Ujung Kulon
National Park),
Indonesia; Vietnam
(Cat Tien National Park)

Otter-civet
p50
North Vietnam and
Cambodia, through
Thailand and
Peninsular Malaysia to
Sumatra and Borneo

Babirusa
p39
Sulawesi and
neighbouring
islands (Indonesia)

Savanna

Tropical rainforest

Mountains

Babirusa

Babyrousa babyrussa

Head/body length: 85–10cm
Height at shoulder: 65–80 cm
Tail length: 27–32cm
Weight: 43–100kg

Fearful face

It's hard to imagine your teeth growing out through your nose. This bizarre arrangement doesn't bother a male babirusa, but it has inspired a variety of demonic ceremonial masks among the islanders who share its home.

Babirusa means 'pig-deer', which indicates the confusion that surrounds this animal. However, its rounded, largely hairless body clearly shows that it belongs to the pig family. The male's curling tusks are upper canine teeth that grow vertically from its snout and bend over towards the forehead, reaching 30cm in length. The equally long lower canines grow out of the mouth and above the upper lip. Youngsters lack the stripes of other piglets and are plain brown, much like adults.

River retreats

The babirusa is endemic to the Indonesian island of Sulawesi and neighbouring Togian, Buru and Sula, where it frequents rainforest and deciduous forest along the banks of rivers and lakes. Once found in coastal areas, it is now increasingly confined to higher, less accessible ground.

There are three distinct subspecies, regarded by some authorities as full species: *B. b. celebensis*, found on mainland Sulawesi, sports large folds of skin around the neck and belly; *B. b. babyrussa*, found on Buru and Sula, has a short hairy coat and is also known as the 'hairy' or 'golden' babirusa; and *B. b. togeanensis* is confined to the Togian Islands. In total only about 5,000 animals remain.

Bare-hoof boxers

Scientists have long struggled to explain the babirusa's outrageous tusks. It seems probable that they help males gauge one another's prowess: rivals will rear up on their hind legs and 'box' tusks with their opponent.

Babirusas are active during the day and have excellent senses of hearing and smell. They feed on fruits, fungi, leaves, insect larvae, nuts and small mammals, though, unlike other pigs, seldom root around with their snouts. Adult males are mostly solitary, while females form small groups. Both are nimble runners, weaving paths through the forest. They enjoy a good mud wallow and are excellent swimmers, capable of reaching offshore islands.

Reproduction is slow for a pig, with females bearing one or two piglets per litter. These are weaned at six to eight months and reach sexual maturity after one to two years. Babirusas live for up to 24 years.

WHERE TO SEE IT

Nantu Forest Reserve on the Paguyaman River, in Sulawesi's little-known province of Gorontalo, is the babirusa's last stronghold. This normally elusive species is regularly seen here, especially when congregating at the Adudu saltlick.

Malaysia

Indonesia

THREATS

Babirusa numbers continue to fall due to illegal poaching and the loss of habitat through logging. Deforestation is doubly disastrous: not only does it destroy the animals' home, it also exposes them to hunters.

186
EDGE RANK

Sumatran rhinoceros

Dicerorhinus sumatrensis

Head/body length: 240–320cm
Height at shoulder: 120–145cm; **Tail length:** 35–60cm
Horn length: 15–25cm (front); **Weight:** 500–800kg

WHERE TO SEE IT

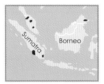

Your chances in the wild are slim. The largest remaining populations are on Sumatra, primarily in Bukit Barisan Selatan and Way Kambas National Parks. In Sabah a handful remain in Tabin Wildlife Reserve and Danum Valley. The Sumatran Rhino Sanctuary in Way Kambas has a captive breeding programme, but this is not open to the public. Otherwise try Cincinnati Zoo, where sightings are guaranteed. Details at: www.rhinos-irf.org; www.savetherhino.org

THREATS

The Sumatran rhino's horn and other body parts have been used in Asian medicine for centuries. Although hunting is now illegal, poachers can still earn high prices. Meanwhile forest clearance for logging and palm oil plantations is the major threat. This even encroaches on national parks, driving rhinos into marginal areas where their small, fragmented populations are left vulnerable to disease.

6
EDGE RANK

Hairy and horny

This rhino, the world's smallest, is sometimes nicknamed 'hairy rhino' from the shaggy coat that it grows in captivity. In the wild, however, the rubbing of forest vegetation keeps the hair on its reddish-brown hide short and bristly, except for longer tufts on the ears and tail. It has two horns, with the small rear one often absent in females, and dagger-like lower incisors used during territorial fights.

Sumatran rhinos live in dense tropical forest, preferring areas with plentiful water and mineral licks. They once ranged across much of Southeast Asia, but today survive only in tiny enclaves in Sumatra, Peninsular Malaysia and Sabah (Borneo). About 300 remain in the wild.

Salt-lick city

This rhino browses on a variety of plants, especially saplings, young leaves and shoots, and has an appetite for wild mangos, bamboo and figs. It forages with its grasping upper lip, munching up to 50kg in an average day.

Each individual has a favourite saltlick, often a muddy seepage of mineral-rich water, that it visits regularly for essential minerals. These sites are where males pick up the scent of receptive females. Otherwise Sumatran rhinos are solitary creatures, except when breeding. Females have stable, partially overlapping home ranges, while males are more nomadic. Both sexes mark their territories with droppings, urine and soil scrapes.

Sumatran rhinos feed at dawn, dusk or after dark, wallowing in mud by day to keep cool and avoid biting insects. They wander a network of forest trails, usually along river courses or ridge tops, which they share with elephants and other species. Excellent hearing and a good sense of smell compensate for their poor eyesight, and are more useful senses in dense forest.

This species lives for around 30–45 years, reaching sexual maturity at six to seven years in females and around ten years in males. Females give birth to a single calf every four to five years.

Javan rhinoceros

Rhinoceros sondaicus

Head/body length: 300–320cm
Height at shoulder: 140–175cm (120cm, Viet race)
Tail length: 70cm
Horn length: 15–20cm
Weight: 1,500–2,300kg (less than 800kg, Viet race)

WHERE TO SEE IT

Ujung Kulon National Park on the Indonesian island of Java is the only place to see this species, but it's not easy. Forest walks may reveal tracks and dung, but the chances of seeing the animal itself are very slim. Details at: www.rhinos-irf.org; www.savetherhino.org

THREATS

This rhinoceros was once common across the region, but severe habitat loss and fragmentation over the centuries have brought about its massive decline. While poaching for its horn and other body parts remains a potential threat, effective protection has meant there has been no known incident since 1993. The extremely small population size also leaves this species vulnerable to disease and possibly to genetic complications caused by inbreeding. In confined areas, competition for food with banteng (indigenous wild cattle) may also pose a threat.

11
EDGE RANK

Armour-plated pachyderm

This species is similar to though slightly smaller than the Indian rhino (see page 26), with the same 'armour-plated' look to its deeply folded skin. Its colour depends on where it's been wallowing, and when wet it can look almost black. Males and females are similar in size, though the Vietnamese subspecies is much smaller than the Indonesian one and in some instances even smaller than the Sumatran rhino. Males have a single horn, while female horns are smaller or absent. Both sexes share the prehensile lip, which is used to grasp foliage.

Preferred habitat is grasslands and reedbeds around dense lowland rainforests. Essential requirements also include a good supply of water, mud wallows and saltlicks for important minerals.

Once widespread in Southeast Asia, the Javan rhino is now confined to two disparate locations: the Indonesian subspecies in Ujung Kulon National Park on Java; and the Vietnamese subspecies at Cat Loc in Cat Tien National Park. This is the rarest rhino and may be the world's rarest mammal, with no more than 60 remaining: most are in Ujung Kulon, with perhaps just eight at Cat Loc.

Mud lark

Like other Asian rhinos, this one is predominantly a browser, using its prehensile upper lip to pluck shoots, twigs, young foliage and fallen fruit – and sometimes to graze grasses. Saltlicks were historically important resources, but in Ujung Kulon there are none and salt-craving rhinos have even been known to drink seawater.

To a Javan rhino mud is certainly glorious, and it spends a large part of most days wallowing. Over time, temporary pools and puddles become deepened and moulded into favourite mud holes. These are essential for keeping cool, maintaining healthy skin and getting rid of parasites.

This is a largely solitary animal, except when breeding. In Ujung Kulon males maintain loose territories of 12–20km², while females have a smaller home range of 3–14 km². They use dung heaps as focal points of communication.

Sumatran rabbit

Nesolagus netscheri

Head/body length: 368–417mm; **Tail length:** 17mm
Ear length: 43–45mm; **Weight:** approx 1.5–2kg

Striped suit

This unusual rabbit sports 'go faster' stripes along its face and body, which are thought to provide camouflage on the forest floor. Otherwise it is similar in size to a European rabbit, with a grey coat, white belly and reddish rump. It has shorter ears than most rabbits and a very small tail.

Home is dense montane forests, with most records being at 600–1,600m in altitude. It is known only from the Barisan Mountains in west and southwest Sumatra, Indonesia, but may also occur in Gunung Leuser and Mount Kerinci National Parks.

No living specimen has been seen since the 1930s and the species was presumed extinct until, miraculously, it was snapped by a camera trap in 1998. Local peoples have no native name for this species, which remains one of the most elusive mammals on the planet.

Squatter bunny

The Sumatran rabbit is completely nocturnal. It appears not to dig its own burrows, but hides during the day in those dug and deserted by other animals. It forages in the understorey for leaves and stalks, never venturing into clearings.

WHERE TO SEE IT

In this case seeing really would be believing. If you manage to catch a glimpse of this rabbit in the Barisan Mountains, you'd be in an exclusive minority of one.

THREATS

Loss of forest habitat to cultivation, especially tea and coffee plantations, underpins all threats to this species.

10 EDGE RANK

Dinagat moonrat

Podogymnura aureospinula

Head/body length: 190–211mm
Tail length: 59–73mm; **Weight:** unknown

Bristle back

This peculiar insectivore has stiff bristly or spiny fur that is golden brown with black speckling on the back. Its belly fur lacks spines and is mostly brownish-grey. The ears are sparsely covered with short white or dark brown hairs.

Also known as the Dinagat gymnure, this species inhabits primary and logged dipterocarp rainforest. Records exist from just three islands in the Philippines: Dinagat, Siargao and Bucas Grande.

An unknown quantity

Scientists know very little about the habits and lifestyle of this species. Hence there are no available images of a live animal (the picture opposite depicts a dead specimen collected by scientists). Close relatives like the common moonrat from the Malay Peninsula, Sumatra and Borneo are strictly nocturnal and live on the forest floor, where they feed on earthworms and other invertebrates. Perhaps the Dinagat moonrat does the same.

WHERE TO SEE IT

As so little is known about this creature it's difficult to suggest exactly where to look. But your search is certainly confined to rainforests on the Philippines islands of Dinagat, Siargao and Bucas Grande.

THREATS

The patches of forest habitat where this species occurs are being rapidly destroyed by logging, slash-and-burn agriculture and mining.

=47 EDGE RANK

Hoolock gibbon

Hylobates hoolock

Head/body length: 60–90cm
Weight: 6–8.5kg (males and females similar)

King of the swingers

Gibbons are apes and, like us, have no tail. Their scientific name *Hylobates* actually means 'dweller in trees' and they are amongst the most agile of canopy dwellers, with arms so long they look like they've been stretched on a rack. These, combined with mobile shoulders and hands that act like hooks, enable them to swing almost effortlessly through the treetops, covering 3m or more in a single swing and topping speeds of 30km/h.

This species is the second largest of the gibbon family. Like all its kind, males and females wear different coloured coats, males being completely black and females golden-brown. Both have dark faces with bushy white eyebrows.

The hoolock gibbon is found in a variety of forest types, including rainforest, mixed deciduous forests and subtropical hill forests. Its range extends from northeast India (Assam, Arunachal Pradesh, Manipur, Meghalaya, Mozoram, Tripura and Nagaland) through to Bangladesh, Myanmar and west Yunnan Province in southwest China.

Canopy songster

Hoolock gibbons mate for life and live in cosy family groups of male, female and dependent offspring. They are very protective of their patch of forest, with territories measuring around 22ha, and are quick to intimidate and chase away intruders.

Few sounds in nature are more evocative than the whooping song of a gibbon resounding through the rainforest. Males and females have different

sounding calls and sing 'romantic' duets that help establish and defend their territories.

This species is active only during the day. It spends most of the time in the treetops, where it often sunbathes – particularly on cold winter mornings – and very rarely descends to the ground. Fruits such as figs dominate its diet, though it will also eat leaves, shoots, insects and even birds' eggs.

Breeding behaviour is little known. It appears that a single offspring is born between November and February. The youngster has grey-white fur tinged with yellow that darkens with age. It stays with its parents until well beyond adolescence.

WHERE TO SEE IT

In Assam, northeast India, you can see hoolock gibbons in Panbari Forest, part of Kaziranga National Park, and also in Manas National Park and Borajan Reserve Forest. For the more adventurous, Namdapha National Park in neighbouring Arunachal Pradesh also offers an opportunity.

THREATS

Inevitably, habitat destruction and fragmentation are at the heart of this species' decline. Many forest areas have been logged or developed into tea plantations. Hunting also poses a serious threat, as gibbon meat and bones are prized locally as food and for use in traditional medicine.

251
EDGE RANK

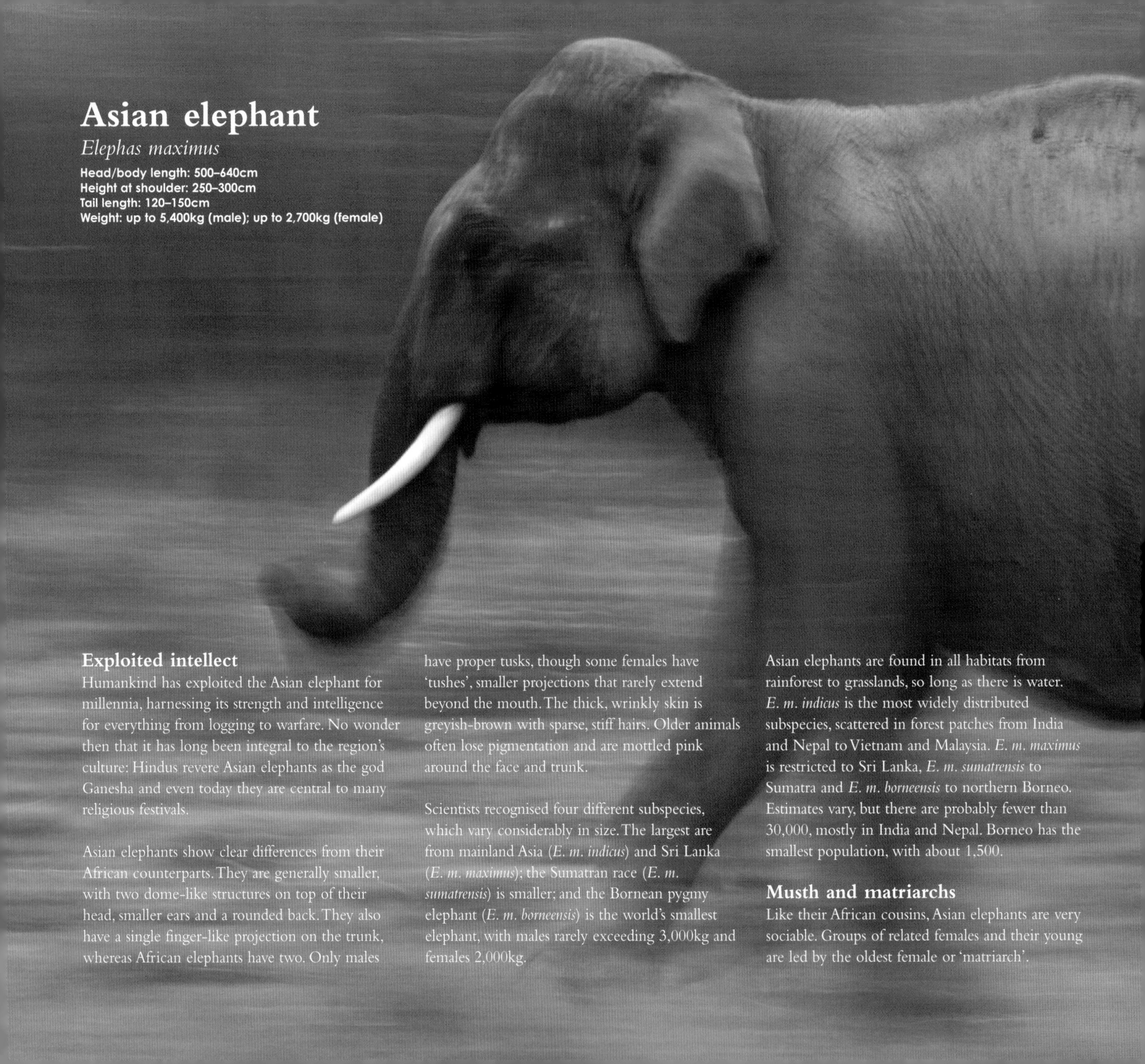

Asian elephant

Elephas maximus

Head/body length: 500–640cm
Height at shoulder: 250–300cm
Tail length: 120–150cm
Weight: up to 5,400kg (male); up to 2,700kg (female)

Exploited intellect

Humankind has exploited the Asian elephant for millennia, harnessing its strength and intelligence for everything from logging to warfare. No wonder then that it has long been integral to the region's culture: Hindus revere Asian elephants as the god Ganesha and even today they are central to many religious festivals.

Asian elephants show clear differences from their African counterparts. They are generally smaller, with two dome-like structures on top of their head, smaller ears and a rounded back. They also have a single finger-like projection on the trunk, whereas African elephants have two. Only males

have proper tusks, though some females have 'tushes', smaller projections that rarely extend beyond the mouth. The thick, wrinkly skin is greyish-brown with sparse, stiff hairs. Older animals often lose pigmentation and are mottled pink around the face and trunk.

Scientists recognised four different subspecies, which vary considerably in size. The largest are from mainland Asia (*E. m. indicus*) and Sri Lanka (*E. m. maximus*); the Sumatran race (*E. m. sumatrensis*) is smaller; and the Bornean pygmy elephant (*E. m. borneensis*) is the world's smallest elephant, with males rarely exceeding 3,000kg and females 2,000kg.

Asian elephants are found in all habitats from rainforest to grasslands, so long as there is water. *E. m. indicus* is the most widely distributed subspecies, scattered in forest patches from India and Nepal to Vietnam and Malaysia. *E. m. maximus* is restricted to Sri Lanka, *E. m. sumatrensis* to Sumatra and *E. m. borneensis* to northern Borneo. Estimates vary, but there are probably fewer than 30,000, mostly in India and Nepal. Borneo has the smallest population, with about 1,500.

Musth and matriarchs

Like their African cousins, Asian elephants are very sociable. Groups of related females and their young are led by the oldest female or 'matriarch'.

WHERE
TO SEE IT

India has several
parks where you can
see wild elephants
relatively easily, including Corbett National
Park in Uttaranchal Pradesh and Kaziranga
National Park in Assam. Other good options
include Bardia National Park in Nepal and
Minneriya National Park in Sri Lanka. Asian
elephants are less easy to see in Indonesia
or Malaysia. However, the Bornean pygmy
elephant can be viewed in the Lower
Kinabatangan Wildlife Sanctuary when
small herds emerge to drink at the water's
edge: their placid temperament allows
boats to approach quite closely and
providing you remain quiet, a long and
fulfilling encounter is possible.

THREATS

Habitat loss has hastened the decline
of the Asian elephant. Vast areas of
forest have been logged or
converted to agriculture, and isolated
elephant populations have become
cut off from their historic migratory
routes by human settlements. This
results in increased elephant-human
conflict, with crops raided, property
destroyed and casualties on both
sides. Poaching for ivory and
occasionally meat also remains a
threat. Since only males have
tusks, some wild populations
end up mostly female, which
badly skews breeding success.

12
EDGE RANK

Strong bonds develop, which are especially helpful in the upbringing of immature animals. In India, female groups can range over 600km², while males typically use 200–400km².

Males leave the family group at around six or seven years to begin a largely solitary life, occasionally forming small 'bachelor' groups. After 20 years bulls reach maturity and annually come into 'musth' – a Hindi/Urdu word meaning 'intoxicated' that describes their extreme state of testosterone-fuelled arousal. Full-grown males can remain this way for around 60 days, constantly on the search for receptive females. Their unpredictable behaviour at this time can make them very dangerous.

Their diet is mostly grasses, with some bark, roots, stems and leaves and vines thrown in. Since many cereal crops are cultivated grasses, it's not surprising that elephants have developed a taste for them – bringing inevitable conflict with farmers and villagers. One individual eats about 170–200kg of food per day, but more than half passes undigested through its inefficient gut. Elephants drink frequently and require 70–90 litres of water daily.

Asian elephants can live for 70 years. Females become sexually mature at around ten, but generally have their first calf at 15–16. If conditions are favourable, they can give birth every three to four years.

Proboscis monkey

Nasalis larvatus

Head/body length: 55–75cm
Tail length: 50–75cm; Weight: 12–23kg, average 20kg
(males); 7–12kg, average 10kg (females)

King conk

Grotesque or endearing? Either way, two features make proboscis monkeys unmistakable: a bizarre pendulous nose and an outrageous pot belly. Both are more pronounced in males and explain the

monkey's local name *Orang Belanda*, or 'Dutchman', as they once reminded indigenous people of early European explorers. Another unusual feature is the partially webbed back feet, which help these monkeys to swim across waterways that are too wide for their prodigious leaps.

Adults are buff-brown with pinkish faces and striking white tails. A mature male has a thick swathe of dark brown fur on the back, like a bomber jacket zipped tightly over his middle-age paunch. Newborn infants have sparse blackish fur, blue faces and snub noses.

Proboscis monkeys are endemic to Borneo, where they inhabit coastal swamp and mangrove forests, sometimes penetrating along riverbanks into the interior of the island.

A bellyful

Proboscis monkeys have a specialised digestive system, including a multi-chambered stomach, which can extract maximum nutrition from their diet of leaves. This stomach contains a cocktail of bacteria to help digest the foliage, which accounts for the pot belly.

The big nose is less easy to explain. Some think it acts like a snorkel, others that it regulates body temperature, but neither idea explains why it is larger in males. A more likely explanation is sex: females fancy males with bigger noses, who consequently produce more offspring than smaller-nosed males, so passing on this advantageous trait to future generations.

Proboscis monkeys have overlapping home ranges of up to 9km². Breeding groups number up to 30, and each comprises a dominant male together with females of all ages and younger males. Separate bachelor groups contain just males. By day they

may travel far, but rarely stray more than 600m from the river. Females kick-start the daily routine, with adult males generally being the last to leave the sleep site. By evening groups have returned to their riverside roost.

These highly vocal primates use their large nose to amplify a noisy repertoire of roars, grunts, groans, squeals and honks. Females initiate mating, normally in February–November, and give birth to a single offspring after a gestation period of around 165 days, eating the placenta after delivery.

WHERE TO SEE IT

Proboscis monkeys are not hard to see in the right places. These include the forest around Sukau on the

Kinabatangan River in Sabah and Bako National Park in Sarawak. At Sukau you can watch monkeys from riverboat trips. In Bako boardwalks through the mangroves allow you to see them foraging on the mudflats or feeding in the trees.

THREATS

Numbers have fallen dramatically in the last 40 years, primarily due to habitat loss. Huge areas of native forest have been cleared for timber and oil palm plantations, and the monkeys cannot adapt to degraded habitat. Hunting is also a problem in places, with the monkeys' sociable behaviour making them easy targets.

375
EDGE RANK

Bumblebee bat
Craseonycteris thonglongyai

Head/body length: 29–33mm
Forearm length: 22–26mm
Weight: 2.2–2.6g

Miniscule mammal

Weighing no more than two drawing pins, this is the world's smallest mammal. It has reddish-brown or grey fur, a swollen, pig-like nose and large ears. Wide wings allow it to hover like a hummingbird, while a pocket of skin between its hind legs acts like a catching glove for insects.

The bumblebee bat inhabits evergreen or deciduous forests near rivers, roosting in caves and hunting over nearby fields. It is known from just two localities: the Khwae Noi River in Sai Yok National Park in western Thailand; and the floodplains of the Thanlwin, Ataran and Gyaing rivers in southeast Myanmar. Fewer than 4,000 are thought to remain.

Flight of the bumblebee bat

Roosts usually number around 100 animals, which spread out across the cave roof. Around dawn and dusk they set out for just 30 minutes to feed, rarely venturing more than 1km from their roost. They hunt small insects on the wing and glean others from leaves. Females are thought to produce a single offspring in late April each year.

WHERE TO SEE IT

You can see these bats emerging at dawn or dusk from any suitable caves within their range. But keep your distance in order to avoid causing any disturbance.

THREATS
Its very restricted distribution makes this species vulnerable. Threats include annual forest burning near roost caves (Thailand) and air pollution from cement factories (Myanmar). **49** EDGE RANK

Palawan stink badger
Mydaus marchei

Head/body length: 320–460mm
Tail length: 10–40mm; **Weight:** 2–2.5kg

Stink with stripes

These aptly named relatives of skunks produce foul-smelling secretions from their anal glands. They are squat, stocky animals, with a brown coat,

a yellowish skullcap and a pale stripe running from the neck to the shoulders. They are smaller and paler than their cousin, the Malay stink badger.

This badger is confined to the Philippine islands of Palawan and Busuanga, where it is believed to live in grassland thickets and cultivated areas.

Probably active both day and night, stink badgers dig shallow burrows ending in a single chamber that they line with bedding. They may also use holes made by other animals. Their strong forepaws and claws make ideal tools for excavating the earthworms and other invertebrates that, along with various fruits, form the bulk of their diet.

WHERE TO SEE IT

Puerto Princesa Subterranean River National Park on the northern coast of Palawan is a good place to try. Night walks are possible and perhaps offer the best chance of a sighting. The badger often visits human settlements for easy food. Details at: www.responsibletravel.com; http://whc.unesco.org/pg.cfm

THREATS
The Philippines as a whole has suffered massive deforestation over the last fifty years. Habitat loss and degradation, coupled with some persecution, are the main reasons this species is under threat. **510** EDGE RANK

East towards Eden

Gehan de Silva Wijeyeratne

▲ Vasco da Gama (c.1469–1524)
opened up trade routes to the east

It is hard today to appreciate just how little the West knew of Southeast Asia when most of the world still lay unmapped. As recently as the 12th century many Europeans still believed that the only way to the East was overland. Others – driven by the greed for gold and slaves – set sail to see whether a route lay southwards, around Africa.

By the 12th century explorers had begun to use the magnetic compass, despite initial concerns that its accuracy would be affected by garlic. The Portuguese, under the royal patronage of King Henry the Navigator, pushed further and further south and eventually Vasco da Gama rounded the Cape, reaching India on 20 May 1498. The way now lay open for sea expeditions further east. However, the Portugese sea charts remained closely guarded.

The scramble for spice

The Portuguese spread eastwards to Malacca in what is now Malaysia, and in 1511 three ships sailed for the Moluccas of Indonesia, famous for their spices. Magellan sold to the Spanish his idea of a shorter crossing to the Spice Islands. He set off in 1519 on his epic circumnavigation of the world, a larger world as it turned out than had ever been imagined. His ship the *Victoria* returned to Seville laden with spices, though Magellan himself was killed in the Philippines. Meanwhile, as Spain and Portugal squabbled over the Spice Islands, the secrets of the charts fell into the hands of both the Venetians and the English. Thus Western science at last arrived at one of the most biodiverse regions in the world.

The 16th–19th centuries saw the Dutch, French, Spanish and British fighting for dominance in Southeast Asia. The Dutch founded the Dutch East India Company and consolidated a hold on the Indonesian islands, while the British founded the British East India Company and controlled Malaysia. Both these colonies, although driven mainly by trade in spices and later plantations, attracted many scientists in search of their

The collectors

Collectors were often men of great wealth who helped drive zoological exploration in Southeast Asia by funding the work of naturalists. The private collection amassed by one collector, Hans Sloane, was eventually to form the nucleus of the British Museum's natural history collection. Albert Seba, an apothecary in Amsterdam, sold his large collection of prints and specimens, to Peter the Great of Russia in 1717, but not before they had been illustrated in Seba's *Thesaurus* and provided valuable documentation of new zoological horizons. The Banks Collection, amassed by Sir Joseph Banks on the first voyage of Captain James Cook, includes specimens collected by many other scientists – including those taken by Dr Gerard Koenig from Thailand, Malaya and India during his tenure in the Danish Service. It remains one of the most important natural history collections from the golden era of zoological exploration.

The *Rafflesia* genus of flowers was named in honour of Thomas Stamford Raffles, founder of Singapore. ▶

Alfred Russel Wallace

The English naturalist Alfred Russel Wallace travelled widely around the Indonesian Archipelago from 1854–62, shipping home a staggering 127,000 specimens of the fauna and flora. But it is for two remarkable scientific theories that he is most celebrated. Like Darwin, Wallace was fascinated by where species came from. In 1858, while in the Moluccas, he penned an article entitled 'On the Tendency of Varieties to Depart Indefinitely from the Original Type', which

▲ Alfred Russel Wallace

succinctly reached conclusions about natural selection that Darwin had been pondering for years. The two men presented their theories jointly in a paper to the Linnean Society in London in 1858 (though neither was present at the time). History has since afforded Darwin the plaudits for the theory of evolution, but *The Origin of Species* would not have been written without Wallace – a fact that Darwin himself gracefully conceded.

Wallace's second insight concerned the distribution of species in Southeast Asia. During his travels he noticed a clear divide running through the Indonesian Archipelago. The birds on Bali, for instance, were definitely of Asian stock, yet those on Lombok, a mere 25km away, were similar to Australian species. The dividing line continued north: to its west on Borneo were monkeys and cats; to its east on islands like Celebes (now Sulawesi) and New Guinea these forms were replaced by marsupials. Wallace had discovered the boundary of two converging continental plates: millions of years earlier the islands had been far apart, but continental drift had subsequently brought them together. This faultline separates two of the planet's great zoogeographical regions, the oriental and Australian. Fittingly, it is today known as Wallace's Line.

new-found zoological treasures. One of Indonesia's British governors was the famous Thomas Stamford Raffles, a gifted administrator and naturalist who subsequently founded Singapore. The largest flower in the world, Rafflesia, bears his name.

The British were especially influential in introducing a love of natural history. Their societies, such as the national chapters of the Royal Asiatic Study, still continue a long tradition of publishing scientific discoveries. However, even today the zoology of Southeast Asia is far from fully documented. New species continue to be discovered, including in 1992 the saola – a large mammal related to oxen but in an entirely new genus. Further studies based on vocalisations and DNA techniques, especially of nocturnal animals, may yet reveal even more.

▲ Big game hunters in Thailand during the 1930s display their young tiger trophy.

Gehan de Silva Wijeyeratne is CEO of Jetwing Eco Holidays. He is one of the best-known wildlife and tourism personalities in Sri Lanka through his activities as a writer and photographer.

Otter-civet

Cynogale bennettii

Head/body length: 57–68cm; Tail length: 12–20cm
Weight: unknown

Big nose

This rather bizarre creature looks like a cross between a mongoose and an otter. Its characteristic features include a pale bulbous muzzle with extremely long whiskers, small ears, webbed feet and a stubby fat tail. Its coat is dark brown with faint grey speckles.

The otter civet frequents rainforests with swamps and rivers. It is found from north Vietnam and Cambodia, through Thailand and Peninsular Malaysia, to Sumatra and Borneo.

Slippery customer

The lifestyle of this little-known species remains shrouded in mystery. We do know, however, that it is a nocturnal animal that lives on the forest floor but hunts in water. Below the surface its sensitive whiskers help to detect prey, which includes fish, crabs and freshwater molluscs. From time to time it may also hunt on land.

WHERE TO SEE IT

Seeing this animal presents a major challenge. One place to try is the peat swamp forest of Pa Phru Toh Daeng (also called Pa Phru Sirindorn) near Sungai Kolok, Thailand. A boardwalk constructed over the wetlands has produced a handful of sightings.

THREATS

Deforestation and the draining of wetland areas are the major threats.

138
EDGE RANK

Bornean bay cat

Catopuma badia

Head/body length: 53–67cm
Height at shoulder: around 28cm
Tail length: 32–39cm; Weight: 2–4kg

Cat on a hat

For more than a century this almost mythical cat eluded most observers. Since the first specimen was collected in 1874 there have been just seven further authentic encounters. In the 1950s a traveller noticed bay cat fur on two ceremonial Dayak hats. Then in 1992 an animal was captured on the Sarawakian–Kalimantan border. A further capture in 1998 allowed the species to be photographed for the first time.

Like a large, leggy domestic cat, the bay cat is rufous-chestnut with faint spots and a creamy belly. Its head is noticeably rounded, with short ears, white facial markings and a distinctive dark 'M' on the head. The long tail has a white tip.

This cat is endemic to Borneo, and probably restricted to the central interior – the so-called 'Heart of Borneo' region. The only records are from dense rainforest, including limestone outcrops and partially logged areas.

WHERE TO SEE IT

Like finding the proverbial needle, only this haystack is the size of Borneo. Celebrity awaits the first person to see and snap a wild bay cat. The latest camera-trap evidence came from Lanjak Entimau Wildlife Sanctuary. It may also occur in Imbak, Maliau Basin and Danum Valley.

THREATS

Although no specific threats have been identified, it is inevitable that the massive deforestation across central Borneo has caused a serious decline in populations.

270
EDGE RANK

Black-crested or black gibbon

Nomascus concolor

Head/body length: 45–64cm
Weight: 5–7kg

WHERE TO SEE IT

Seeing such an elusive and endangered species is a real achievement. The majority of the remaining black-crested gibbons live in forest pockets in China. Gaoligong, Wuliang and Ailao Mountain nature reserves in Yunnan Province offer the best opportunities to track the Yunnan black gibbon, while Bawangling National Nature Reserve on Hainan Island is the only place to see that island's endemic subspecies. In Bokeo Nature Reserve, Laos, you can stay in canopy tree houses and cross between trees on zip wires while looking for gibbons. You might not see them but should at least hear them. There is also a rehabilitation project where gibbons can be seen. Details at: www.gibbonx.org

THREATS

Gibbon species throughout Southeast Asia have suffered dramatic declines due principally to habitat loss and to a lesser extent hunting. Black-crested gibbons have suffered more than most, as around 75% of their original habitat has already gone.

349
EDGE RANK

Boy or girl?

There's no mistaking the gender in this species, as males and females look very different. Males are almost completely black, sometimes with white or buff cheeks, while females are golden or buff with variable black patches, including a black streak on the head. Both sexes have the tuft of longer fur on the crown that gives the species its name.

This gibbon lives in tropical, evergreen broadleaved forests and semi-deciduous monsoon forests. Its range has been greatly reduced and is now restricted to Laos, Vietnam and Yunnun Province in China. Scientists have identified as many as five different subspecies from various parts of its range. One of these, the Hainan black-crested gibbon (*N. c. hainanus*) from Hainan Island, China, is often cited as the world's most endangered primate.

Dawn duets

The black-crested gibbon, like all its kind, is supremely adapted for treetop life and renowned for swinging between the branches on its long arms – a means of locomotion known as brachiation. It eats a variety of ripe sugary fruit such as figs, and less frequently leaves and insects.

Small family groups each comprise a monogamous pair and their offspring. With the female taking the lead, the pair regularly sing together in the morning, producing a variety of calls that they amplify with the aid of a throat sac. These duets are essential for reinforcing pair bonds and also help in defending territory.

A female gives birth to single young every two to three years, which is usually weaned at two years.

Orang-utan (Bornean and Sumatran)

Pongo pygmaeus (Bornean orang-utan)
Pongo abelii (Sumatran orang-utan)

Head/body length: 1.25–1.50m; **Arm span:** 2.25m
Weight: 70–130kg (male); 30–55kg (female)

Orang-utan is Malay for 'man of the forest', and this animal's habitat comprises lowland rainforest, riverine forest and swamp forest. Although they once ranged as far as China, today they are restricted to the islands of Borneo and Sumatra. These two populations in fact constitute two separate species: the Sumatran orang-utan is found at the northern tip of Sumatra; the Bornean is restricted to scattered sites in Kalimantan, Sarawak and Sabah. Numbers are hard to estimate: perhaps 7,000 left in Sumatra and 50,000 in Borneo.

Kings of the canopy

The orang-utan is the world's largest tree-dwelling animal. Its forearms are 30% longer than its legs, and both the hands and feet are equally adept at gripping. Individuals clamber around the canopy and can hang upside down from both feet. They cannot jump, but instead span gaps by swinging a tree back and forth until they can reach adjacent branches. Heavy males must sometimes descend to the ground in order to scale the next tree.

Fruit dominates their diet and around half the day is spent feeding. Wild figs are a particular favourite and an individual may remain in a fruiting tree for a day or more, gorging itself. Other food includes leaves, bark, honey, insects and even birds' eggs. Orang-utans help maintain their forest habitat by dispersing seeds and opening up the canopy to allow light to reach the forest floor.

Great red ape

The orang-utan is the ultimate wildlife emblem of Southeast Asia's jungles. It is the only great ape found outside Africa, and its compelling facial expressions and thoughtful, emotion-filled eyes have an instant appeal.

Both sexes have long reddish-orange hair. Colour differs between individuals and changes with age: juveniles may be bright orange, while some old animals are dark chocolate-brown. The face is always bare, and paler in younger animals. Adult males have inflatable throat sacs, which amplify their calls, and fatty cheek pads that become a fleshy facial disc in mature animals. These are more pronounced in Bornean orang-utans.

▲ *Sumatran orang-utan (female)*

Adults lead solitary lives and forage over large areas to find their widely scattered food. They travel about 1km per day, but will move further to find seasonal fruit. Except for mating pairs and females with young, orang-utans meet only if two or more find the same, large fruit-laden tree. Sleeping in the canopy poses problems for such a heavyweight, so each day orang-utans build a nest, bending branches into a sleeping platform up to 1m across. In a torrential downpour, they will also hold a large leaf above their head as an umbrella.

Females start breeding at 12–15 years. Males become sexually mature at the same age, but are not yet old enough to gain access to receptive females. A receptive female may attract several suitors, but she will only accept dominant males with fully developed cheek flanges. These males signify their dominance with 'long calls', which start with a grunting and build to a roar-like crescendo accompanied by a shaking of branches and are audible from a kilometre away.

A single offspring is born every seven to eight years. The female carries it around and they sleep together in the mother's nest until she has her next one. Youngsters may not become completely independent for up to ten years. Life expectancy in the wild is 45–50. A female that lives this long will still produce no more than four surviving offspring. This is the slowest breeding rate of any terrestrial mammal and a major reason why populations recover so slowly.

WHERE TO SEE IT

Seeing orang-utans at rehabilitation centres is straightforward: in Sumatra visit Bukit Lawang outside Gunung Leuser National Park; in Borneo visit Sepilok Orang-utan Rehabilitation Centre (Sabah), Matang Wildlife Centre (Sarawak) or Tanjung Puting National Park (Central Kalimantan). For truly wild sightings try Danum Valley or the Lower Kinabatangan Wildlife Sanctuary (Sabah), or – for the more adventurous – Tanjung Puting. At the latter you must join a trip led by members of research staff. Details at: www.orangutan.org; www.orangutans-sos.org; www.orangutan.com

THREATS

Massive deforestation has devastated orang-utan populations over the past 200 years. This continues today as logging and conversion to agriculture, in particular oil palm plantations, gathers pace. At this rate orang-utans may become extinct in the wild within the next 10–20 years. Infants are sometimes seized for the illegal pet trade, with as many as three adults killed for each one that is successfully captured. Their low reproductive rate leaves orang-utans especially vulnerable to all such threats.

97
EDGE RANK

Pygmy hog
Sus salvanius

Head/body length: 61–71cm (male); 55–62cm (female)
Height at shoulder: 20–30cm
Tail length: 2–3cm
Weight: 8–10kg (males); 6–8kg (female)

pink, but after ten days the pygmy porkers develop a brown coat with pale yellow-ochre stripes that is so characteristic of wild pig young.

The pygmy hog lives in dense, tall grasslands and mixed scrub on large river floodplains. It was once found in suitable habitats at the southern foothills

single file along well-worn trails through tall grass, keeping in touch with one another using soft grunts. Like most wild pigs, pygmy hogs eat anything from roots, grasses and fruits, to insects, earthworms and other invertebrates.

In the mating season, from late November, rival males battle it out over females using elaborate threat displays. Females move away from their group to give birth and a typical litter is four to six piglets. Both sexes scrape nests in the soil and line them with dry grass.

Tiny trotter

This tiny trotter is a double record-holder: it is both the world's smallest and most endangered wild pig. Indeed it was once feared extinct until being 'rediscovered' in 1971.

Adults have a compact, rounded frame, and are grey-brown along the back and sides but paler underneath. The covering of coarse hair is particularly long behind the shoulders and forms a cute crest on their forehead. Piglets are born greyish

of the Himalayas, from northern India through Bhutan to Nepal. Today it lives only in Manas National Park and Barnadi Wildlife Sanctuary in Assam, where just 100–150 are thought to survive.

Indian file

Males and females adopt quite different ways of life. Males are loners and keep to themselves, whereas female and young band together in small groups called 'sounders'. Their small home ranges cover about 25ha. When foraging, they walk in

WHERE TO SEE IT

Bhutan

India

Manas National Park in northwest Assam is the only place you're likely to see the pygmy hog, but because numbers are so low this remains a difficult proposition. The best time to visit is January–April, and elephant-back safaris are the most exciting way to see wildlife. The park is a six-hour drive from Guwahati, and there are lodges and forest resthouses to stay in.

THREATS

The pygmy hog's tall grassland habitat has suffered widespread destruction by burning to make way for agriculture and domestic grazing stock. Even within the bounds of Manas National Park there is human encroachment and periodic political unrest in the area hampers ongoing conservation efforts.

=134
EDGE RANK

Pygmy slow loris

Nycticebus pygmaeus

Head/body length: 18–21cm; Tail length: virtually none
Weight: 400–450g

Cute and cuddly

With its huge eyes and fluffy fur, the pygmy slow loris looks like a tiny teddy bear. It has a round head, small ears and short, sturdy limbs. Muscular hands and feet give it a tight grip on branches.

Home for this creature is tropical dry forests, ranging from Vietnam and Laos to parts of south China and Cambodia.

Toxic teeth

Pygmy slow lorises are nocturnal and solitary. They curl up for the day in a tree hole, then set out foraging after dark, clambering deliberately along branches in search of prey. When they spot a meal, they grip tightly with their hind feet and lunge for the prize with their hands.

Their diet includes fruits and small animals and invertebrates. Amazingly, this loris subdues prey using a poisonous bite, which it gets by licking a toxic secretion from glands on the inside of its elbows. Its teeth also have a comb-like structure, used for scraping resin from tree bark.

WHERE TO SEE IT
Among various reserves in Vietnam, Cat Tien National Park, three hours drive from Ho Chi Minh City, is the best option and offers night walks and night drives. Use an infrared light to minimise disturbance. Details at: www.loris-conservation.org

Malaysia

Indonesia

THREATS
The Vietnam war nearly wiped out this species by destroying its forests. The destruction continues today, making way for agriculture and development.

200
EDGE RANK

Visayan warty pig

Sus cebifrons

Head/body length: 115–125cm (males); 90–100cm (females); Weight: 35–40kg (males); 25–30kg (females)

Floppy fringe

A floppy fringe and warty face give this pig cartoon-character looks. Boars are much larger than sows, with tusks. Both have pale bristly hair, a dark muzzle and, during the breeding season, a long crest and mane.

Historically this species was found throughout the Visayan Islands (the central archipelago of the Philippines), but it has now disappeared from at least 98% of its former range. Surviving populations are confined to scattered rainforest fragments on the islands of Negros and the western mountains of Panay.

Crop raiders

Little is known about this pig. It lives in groups of four to six animals, although solitary males are also seen. Food comprises various forest fruits, roots and tubers, but also includes crops – increasingly so as native forests shrink.

Piglets are born in the dry season between January and March. The small litter of just one to three grows very slowly.

WHERE TO SEE IT
On Negros you can see pigs in Mount Canlaon National Park and Panay Mountains National Park. The Visayan Warty Pig Conservation Programme runs captive breeding centres on both islands, which provide easier though more artificial sightings.

Philippines

Panay·
Negros

THREATS
Widespread deforestation and heavy hunting are significant and ongoing threats. Also, interbreeding with domestic pigs is rapidly undermining the integrity of surviving purebred populations.

=134
EDGE RANK

Conserving Southeast Asia's wildlife

Southeast Asia today presents an environmental paradox, with some of the world's most densely populated urban areas sitting alongside some of its most remote and unexplored wild places. Rapid development and deforestation are eroding the region's habitats at an alarming rate, and even as new animal species continue to be discovered, their forest home is shrinking around them.

Razed to the ground: *Slash-and-burn threatens forests across Southeast Asia.* ▲

Logging out

Deforestation is a critical conservation issue in Southeast Asia, as with tropical rainforest the world over. Over 90% of the original forest cover in the Philippines, for instance, has already gone, while forest cover in Indonesia as a whole has fallen from 162 million to 98 million hectares in the last 50 years alone. Unsustainable commercial logging, both legal and illegal, is the driving force behind this destruction across most of the region, although burning forest to clear land for development and agriculture – such as palm oil plantations – is also prevalent. Among the consequences are the displacement of indigenous forest peoples, flash flooding, drought and air pollution, and the wholesale devastation of forest ecosystems.

The orang-utan, now found only in Borneo and Sumatra, is the flagship species for the plight of Southeast Asian forests, with logging and forest fires having wiped out 80% of its habitat in the last 20 years. The World Wildlife Fund (*www.wwf.org.uk*) has been involved in the conservation of orang-utans since 1962. A key part of its work is in the conservation of an area known as the 'Heart of Borneo', which comprises 220,000km² of largely untouched equatorial rainforest straddling the island's three administrative regions. WWF is working with the Indonesian, Malaysian and Bruneian governments to establish protected areas here under sustainable management. Other species set to benefit include the Bornean clouded leopard and the Sumatran rhinoceros.

Caught on camera

Many of the elusive forest animals of Southeast Asia are very poorly known and documented. However, the innovative use of heat- or movement-triggered cameras has enabled scientists to get an intimate look at many species rarely or never observed before. The Sumatran striped rabbit

▲ Snap happy: *Camera traps have given scientists many insights into rainforest wildlife.*

had not been seen in the wild since 1916 until it was caught on camera in 1998. The following year, a new species, the Annamite striped rabbit, was photographed in the forests of Laos after specimens were found on sale in local markets, while on Borneo a WWF camera trap famously took the first-ever photograph of a wild Sumatran rhinoceros in 2006. Research funded by the International Otter Survival Fund (www.otter.org) used camera traps to establish the presence of the endangered hairy-nosed otter in Vietnam, and Save the Tiger Fund (www.savethetigerfund.org) has recently been involved in funding camera-trap projects on the distribution, population and movements of tigers in Malaysia.

Tigers probably disappeared from Borneo during prehistoric times. The two unique subspecies of tiger on Bali and Java, however, both became extinct within the last century, while the south China tiger may now also be extinct in the wild. The 1,000 or so tigers that remain in the region occupy shrinking habitat patches, forcing them into dangerous proximity with human habitation. Meanwhile poachers continue to hunt these magnificent animals illegally in order to supply the lucrative market in traditional Chinese medicine. The Sumatran Tiger Conservation Programme (*www.tigertrust.info/ stcp.htm*), funded exclusively by the Sumatran Tiger Trust, has already undertaken extensive research to gain a clear picture of the ecological needs of this race, and now works with land managers and law enforcers to safeguard the 350 tigers on the island.

After the flood

The tsunami of 26 December 2004 caused widespread loss of life and destruction across coastal areas of Southeast Asia. The damage was worst along coastlines, such as those of Sumatra, that were already degraded by the loss of coral reefs and mangrove forests. The Green Coast Project (*www.wetlands.org/greencoast/en*) is an initiative co-ordinated by Wetlands International that aims to assess damage to coastal wetlands and to integrate the rebuilding of local communities with measures to restore the damaged habitats.

Re-establishing ecologically sound land use and ecotourism in tsunami-hit regions is a key conservation issue, and several ecotourism companies now offer an opportunity to become involved. For example, www.responsible

Dolphin dedication

Species isolated within a single threatened habitat require dedicated conservation efforts. The Mekong River in Laos and Cambodia is home to a small, isolated population of the endangered Irrawaddy dolphin. Although this faces numerous threats, including overfishing, entanglement in gill nets and noise harassment from boat traffic, the Mekong Dolphin Conservation Project (*www.mekongdolphin.org/*) is optimistic that conservation measures can be effective and has devised a detailed action plan to help.

▲ **Sold down the river:** Irrawaddy dolphins, like other freshwater cetaceans, need urgent conservation help.

travel.com has developed holidays to Sri Lanka and Thailand that include some time working with affected communities as well as visits to national parks. In the wake of such devastation, it is encouraging to see how many organisations and communities are taking the opportunity to address the needs of the environment as they put their recovery plans into place.

◄ **An eye for danger:** Sumatran tigers frequently come into conflict with human interests as their habitat shrinks.
◄ **Save our skins:** Trade in animal parts continues to drive illegal hunting of endangered species.
◄ **Road to recovery:** A rescued orang-utan awaits its return to the wild at a rehabilitation centre on Borneo.

Australasia

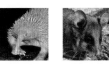

The island continent of Australia dominates the Australasian region, which also includes New Zealand, Melanesia, other Pacific islands and New Guinea. Due to its long isolation, following the break-up of the Gondwana 'supercontinent', the region is a refuge for relic mammals whose ancestors first evolved over 100 million years ago. These evolved into a spectacular variety of forms once the dinosaurs died out some 35 million years later.

Today Australasia is home to the majority of the world's marsupials, or 'pouched' mammals, and all the monotremes, or 'egg-laying' mammals. The marsupials, especially, have radiated extravagantly to occupy most available ecological niches in the region. There are numerous examples of parallel evolution, whereby Australasian forms take the parts played by placental mammals in other parts of the world – for instance, kangaroos occupying the role of deer, antelope and other grazing ungulates.

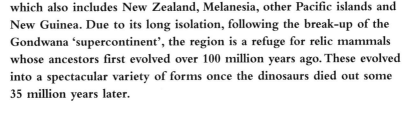

The arrival of humans in the Australasian region 60,000–50,000 years ago precipitated a profound effect on its fauna and flora. Firstly, from 13,000–9,000 years ago the early colonists hunted many large mammals to extinction. Then with later, successive waves of human invasion came dogs, pigs, goats, rabbits and rodents. All have contributed in their own ways to the decline or disappearance of numerous native species.

◀ *Leadbeater's possum is the only non-gliding member of the Petauridae, a distinctive family of possums noted for their gliding.*

Black-spotted cuscus
p64
Northern
New Guinea

Long-beaked echidna
p62
New Guinea and offshore islands, from PNG to Irian Jaya

0   500 km   1000 km   1500 km
0   500   1000 miles

Mediterranean scrub

Semidesert

Desert

Wetland

Steppe (grass, brush and thicket)

Savanna

Woodland savanna

Tropical rainforest

Temperate and montane grassland

Mountains

New Guinea

Western barred bandicoot
p64
Bernier and Dorre Islands, Western Australia

Proserpine rock wallaby
p71
Whitsunday Shire, Queensland, Australia

Great Barrier Reef

Lesser New Zealand short-tailed bat
p70
Scattered sites on North Island, South Island and outlying islands, New Zealand

Northern Territory

Great Sandy desert

Western Australia

Queensland

South Australia

New South Wales

Darling

Great Dividing Range

Murray

Victoria

Long-footed potoroo
p61
Scattered sites in Victoria and New South Wales, southeast Australia

Southern marsupial mole
p65
Central Australia: Northern Territory, Western Australia and South Australia

Leadbeater's possum
p69
Central Highlands, Victoria, Australia

Tasmania

Mountain pygmy possum
p68
Scattered sites in Australian Alps, southeast Australia

New Zealand

Long-footed potoroo

Potorous longipes

Head/body length: 380–415mm
Tail length: 315–325mm
Weight: 1.6–2.2kg

WHERE TO SEE IT

NSW

Victoria

Core populations of this species are found in two separate areas in Victoria. Two sub-populations occur within Snowy River National Park, where you can arrange spotlit night-time walks to look for them. Details at: www.parkweb.vic.gov.au. There is also a small captive breeding population at Healesville Sanctuary, a facility set up to research the behaviour and reproduction of species that are difficult to observe in the wild.

THREATS

Much of the long-footed potoroo's very restricted range is subject to logging and associated road construction. Its habitat is becoming increasingly fragmented, which allows easier access for introduced predators such as feral dogs and foxes. Wildfires and logging regimes are also responsible for depleting the potoroo's favourite fungi food.

70
EDGE RANK

Pocket kangaroo

Potoroos look a little like pocket-sized kangaroos and are sometimes called 'rat-kangaroos'. The long-footed potoroo is about the size of a rabbit, with a conical face and a long rat-like tail. Its soft fur is mainly grey-brown but paler on the stomach and feet. It has long back feet, as you might expect, and long toes equipped with strong claws.

This species occurs in a variety of forest types, ranging from wet montane forests at above 1,000m to lowland forest at 150m, but prefers areas that are permanently wet. Dense undergrowth is also important as this provides shelter and protection from predators.

An Australian endemic, the long-footed potoroo has a very restricted range. The two main populations occur in the Barry Mountains and East Gippsland, both in Victoria. A third, smaller population is found in the southeast forests of New South Wales.

Fungal forager

This shy, nocturnal creature spends the day sleeping in a simple nest scraped in the ground, usually in a patch of dense vegetation. It feeds mainly on various underground fungi, which is why it can live only in very moist habitats where this food flourishes. Fruit and some invertebrates sometimes top up the diet.

There is a delicate balance here to maintain. The potoroo's favourite fungus supplies nutrients to trees in the forest, which helps them resist disease. The potoroo then spreads fungal spores through the forest in its dung, and in so doing plays an essential role in keeping the forest healthy.

Breeding takes place throughout the year, but most young are born in the winter, spring and early summer. Females give birth to a single young. They are capable of producing up to three per year, though one or two is the norm.

Long-beaked echidna

Zaglossus bruijni

Head/body length: 450–775mm; Weight: 10kg

WHERE TO SEE IT

Your best chance of seeing a long-beaked echidna is in Lorentz National Park or alternatively in the Arfak Mountains, Tamrau Selatan or Salawati Utara nature reserves. You will need patience and persistence to find them after dark.

THREATS

Traditional hunting is the main reason why these animals are declining. Long-beaked echidnas are highly prized as food by local people, who hunt them with trained dogs. The other major threat comes from habitat destruction in the form of farming, logging and mining. The good news is that Attenborough's long-beaked echidna, not seen since 1961 and presumed extinct, was rediscovered in the Cyclops Mountains in June 2007.

2

EDGE RANK

Ancient line

Looking rather like a large squashed hedgehog with a piece of hosepipe for a nose, the long-beaked echidna is about as strange as mammals get. And even stranger, it lays eggs! This bizarre creature belongs to an extremely ancient group of egg-laying mammals called monotremes, which have changed little in the past 100 million years.

A long-beaked echidna's downcurved snout takes up two-thirds the length of its head. It has no teeth; instead it hooks prey on its spiky tongue and 'reels'

it in. Spines and sparse brownish-black hairs cover its squat body, which is equipped with strong limbs and claws for digging.

High heaven

Long-beaked echidnas are endemic to New Guinea and a few offshore islands, where they inhabit montane rainforests and high alpine meadows. They range from Papua New Guinea in the east to Irian Jaya in the west.

Recent changes in classification now mean three distinct species are recognised: *Z.bruijni* is found in the far west of the island (Vogelkop and Fak Fak mountains); *Z. attenboroughi* is known from a single mountain peak in the Cyclops Mountains; and

Z. bartoni is found in a swathe along the centre.

Pouched eggs

We know little about how these mysterious creatures live. They are largely nocturnal and spend the day in burrows or hollow logs. At night they forage in leaf litter on the forest floor. Their diet consists almost entirely of earthworms, although they sometimes eat termites and ants – hence their alternative name, 'spiny anteater'.

Echidnas are solitary and come together only to breed. A female lays four to six eggs into her pouch each July. These hatch ten days later and the young then remain in the pouch for a further six to seven weeks. There are no teats; instead the youngsters lap from 'milk patches' inside the pouch. They leave the pouch once their spines develop.

When threatened, an echidna erects its spines while simultaneously burrowing into soft ground to protect its belly. On hard ground it curls into a spiky ball like a hedgehog.

Western barred bandicoot

Perameles bougainville

Head/body length: approx. 18cm
Tail length: approx. 10cm; **Weight:** 190–250g

Stripy rump

Bandicoots are small, rat-like marsupials with pointed faces and rabbit-like ears. This species has alternating dark and pale bands across its hindquarters. The female's pouch faces backwards to stop dirt getting in while digging.

Today the western barred bandicoot is restricted to sand hills, grasslands and scrublands. Formerly found over much of southern and western Australia, it was believed extinct until two populations were discovered in the 1970 on Bernier and Dorre islands off the west coast.

A scheme to reintroduce them to the mainland is now under consideration.

Bad neighbours

This solitary, nocturnal creature builds a nest in a scrape lined with leaves and digs around for invertebrates, seeds, roots and herbs. Individuals tend to be rather intolerant of one another and often scrap. But occasionally two are seen to nest together – presumably a male and female.

One to three tiny young are born just 12 days after mating – one of the shortest gestation periods of any mammal. The young stay in the pouch for 45–60 days and are fully independent by 80 days.

WHERE TO SEE IT

Western barred bandicoots remain relatively common on Bernier Island and on Dorre Island's White Beach. Night-time searches amongst the dune scrub should prove successful.

THREATS

Predation by introduced foxes and feral cats has caused the shocking decline of this species. Introduced livestock and rabbits have made things even worse.

202 EDGE RANK

Black-spotted cuscus

Spilocuscus rufoniger

Head/body length: 58–70cm
Tail length: 45–60cm; **Weight:** 5.5–6.6kg

Telling tails

Cuscuses are mainly nocturnal, possum-like marsupials that are very woolly and cute-looking. Their strong prehensile tail, which, bare at the tip, resembles a length of rope. The black-spotted cuscus is the largest species, with females generally larger than males. It has a dense black-and-rufous coat with bushy white cheek patches.

◀ *White-spotted cuscus: a close, less endangered relative*

Other features include a short snout, large eyes and small ears virtually hidden beneath the thick fur. The hands and feet are equipped with sharp curved claws for climbing. Females have a well-developed, forward-opening pouch.

This species is restricted to isolated patches of undisturbed forest in northern New Guinea. It is nowhere common, and thought to be extinct in the east of its range.

Canopy courtship

This is a slow-moving, solitary, acorn-eating tree dweller that occasionally descends to the ground. Courtship takes place in the canopy. Newborn young are protected in the mother's pouch.

WHERE TO SEE IT

Sightings are so rare that advice is hard to give. The mountains of northern New Guinea are remote and only the most adventurous should try. If you fancy your luck, head for the remote Yapsiei area in Sandaun Province.

THREATS

Long prized by Papuans for its meat and coat, this species has vanished from many areas. Firearms have made hunting easier. Habitat loss is also a major factor.

175 EDGE RANK

Southern marsupial mole

Notoryctes typhlops

Head/body length: 90–180mm
Tail length: 12–26mm; **Weight:** 40–65g

WHERE TO SEE IT

This animal's subterranean lifestyle makes sightings exceedingly rare.

Even its tracks are well covered and hard to locate. A research project has been under way since 1999 in the Anangu Pitjantjatjara Yankunytjatjara lands of northern South Australia. It has also been recorded in Uluru (Ayers Rock-Mt Olga) National Park. You should report any positive signs of marsupial mole activity to appropriate authorities. Find helpful hints on how to identify tracks and what to record at: www.marsupialsociety.org/mole_patrol.html. Contact Jarrad Holmes at the Threatened Species Network: emailto:jholmes@wwf.org.au

THREATS

Marsupial moles are prized for their luxuriant golden fur and numbers probably declined sharply in the early 20th century when indigenous peoples traded thousands of pelts with Europeans. Today heavy predation by introduced foxes, feral cats and dingoes is a more pressing concern.

=30
EDGE RANK

Stiff neck

It might resemble your common or garden mole, but this weird creature is more closely related to kangaroos than the animal responsible for ruining your lawn. And while it does share some features with other marsupials, it is not particularly closely allied to them either.

Marsupial moles are Australia's only specialised burrowing mammals. They have powerful forelimbs

and streamlined bodies that are well suited to burrowing through the sandy soil they inhabit. Huge flat claws are adapted for digging, while a protective horny plate shields the snout and fused vertebrae help stiffen their neck for rigidity.

With such a lifestyle these animals have little need for sight or hearing, so their eyes have become non-functional and their external ears have disappeared completely. The female's pouch even opens to the rear to prevent the youngsters from being covered with earth when she is burrowing.

This species is slightly larger than the northern marsupial mole. Its short, velvety fur is generally cream or golden, sometimes tinged pinkish by iron traces in the sand.

Sand dune central

The southern marsupial mole inhabits sand dunes and areas with sandy soils along river flats and has been recorded from the central deserts of the Northern Territory, Western Australia, and northern South Australia.

Underground movement

This species spends most of its time tunnelling just below the surface and only occasionally ventures above the ground. Its horny nose acts like a snowplough and pushes through sandy soil, while its fore-claws scoop sand out of the way and its rear feet shovel it behind. The tunnel collapses behind it as it travels.

Marsupial moles are active both day and night – daylight makes no difference underground – and feed on a variety of prey, including insect larvae, beetles and occasionally small reptiles. They probably breed in November and the young move into their mother's backwards-facing pouch immediately after birth.

Discovering the lands down under

Stella Martin

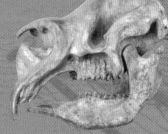

▲ *Diprotodon (back), Palorchestes (centre) and Zygomatrus (front): Australian mammals of the Pleistocene (painting by Michael Long).*

Australia is on the move, rafting north at the rate of 6cm a year (the rate at which a human hair grows). Once it was part of a supercontinent called Gondwana but this started to split up over 150 million years ago: South America, India and Africa made an early bid for independence; the landmass that was to become the New Zealand islands and New Caledonia split next; and finally Australia made the break from Antarctica.

Each of these landmasses carried with it a Gondwanan inheritance, a stock of plants and animals that had evolved in southern latitudes, then much warmer than today's chilly polar regions. These developed in remarkably different ways. In New Caledonia, poor soils saw the evolution of a heath-type vegetation (its superficial similarity to the Scottish Highlands inspiring Captain James Cook's choice of name), as well as abundant insects and reptiles. New Zealand became the land of birds: with no mammals other than three species of bat, many lost the power of flight and behaved as mammals do elsewhere.

Marsupials (mammals with pouches) initially dominated Australia's fauna. Modern placental animals, notably rats and bats, arrived later from Asia, after Australia had pushed up

Acclimatisation societies

In the 1860s acclimatisation societies were established in Australia and New Zealand with the aim of introducing non-native animals. Some, such as songbirds, were intended simply to make homesick colonialists feel at home. Others were just bizarre choices: monkeys once played in the streets of Hobart, their introduction defended 'for the amusement of the wayfarer who their gambols would delight as he lay under some gum-tree in the forest on a sultry day'. Fortunately, they failed to thrive, unlike Australian possums, introduced to New Zealand in 1848 for the fur trade, which have now multiplied to over 60 million and eat an estimated 20,000 tonnes of vegetation a night, stripping forests and spreading disease.

against the Asian plate and created a stepping stone – the island of New Guinea. The traffic was two-way, with marsupials moving north from Australia into New Guinea and pursuing a very different evolutionary future in this mountainous land.

The first migrants

One significant mammal was missing from Australasia until, 60,000–40,000 years ago, some island-hopping humans found their way to Australia, New Guinea and the Solomon Islands. These pioneers would have encountered a trusting fauna, unused to such predators. Arthur Bowes Smyth, in 1788 one of the first humans to land on Lord Howe Island, which lies between New Zealand and Australia, described birds: 'walking totally fearless and unconcern'd … we had nothing more to do than to stand still … and knock down as many as we pleas'd'.

The first Australians would also have found great herds of diprotodons – naive, rhino-sized herbivores resembling enormous wombats. These became extinct about 40,000–20,000 years ago. Among more than 50 other large mammals to go the same way were 'charismatic megafauna' such as giant kangaroos, echidnas the size of sheep, marsupial tapirs and ferocious marsupial lions. Whether their demise was due to human hunting, fire, climate change or a combination of these factors is hotly contested, but a similar pattern can be seen elsewhere in Australasia.

▲ *Moa among kiwis, from a 19th-century print*

In New Caledonia the giant horned turtles, crocodiles and goannas became extinct soon after the arrival of humans about 3,500 years ago. In New Zealand, discovered by Maori just 800–1,000 years ago, the magnificent moas – giant birds reaching up to 3m and weighing a hefty 250kg – were gone within a few hundred years.

The European invasion

Europeans suspected the existence of a southern continent. During the 16th–17th centuries, Portuguese, Spanish and Dutch navigators reached first New Guinea and then charted parts of the Australian coast. Those who encountered the arid west Australian coast were somewhat unimpressed: Rottnest Island (near Perth) was dismissively named in 1696 by a Dutch captain who had mistaken the resident marsupial quokkas for rats.

Background: Repairs being carried out on Cook's ship, the Endeavour

Later explorers took more interest in the wildlife. Marooned in north Queensland for 48 days in 1770 for ship repairs, James Cook and Joseph Banks described the first kangaroo – Banks attributing the name to a local Aboriginal man (although, since the word is unknown in local languages, it has been suggested that Banks was simply being told to get lost). On his arrival in Australia in 1838, gifted British naturalist John Gould found '…objects as strange as if I had been transported to another planet…'. Thus inspired, he set about describing and illustrating the native birds and mammals, and his books were to engender a whole new appreciation for the wildlife of the Antipodean lands.

The perplexing platypus

When the dried skin of a platypus was sent to England in 1798 it was regarded as a hoax, created by devious taxidermists. George Shaw of the British Museum described: '…the perfect resemblance of the beak of a Duck engrafted on the head of a quadruped' and attempted to unpick the stitches with scissors. Australian observations that this bizarre mammal also laid eggs were not accepted by British scientists until 1884 and it was well into the 20th century before the electro-sensory nature of its bill was discovered.

Early painting of platypus by John Gould ▲

*Born in Belfast, **Stella Martin** developed the travel bug early, living and working in Amsterdam, Tokyo, England and Malaysia before settling in Australia. Since the early 1990s she has been employed by the Environmental Protection Agency as a natural history writer.*

Mountain pygmy possum

Burramys parvus

Head/body length: 100–130mm
Tail length: 130–160mm; Weight: 30–60g

Pygmy at large

Although undeniably small, this mouse-like marsupial is the largest member of the pygmy-possum family. Its soft dense fur is brownish-grey on the back and pale cream underneath, with the male's belly turning fawn-orange during the breeding season. The long, virtually naked tail is prehensile, and can get a good grip on twigs and branches. Females have a distinct pouch.

Found at altitudes of 1,500–1,800m, this species inhabits rocky scree slopes and boulder fields amongst alpine and sub-alpine grasses and shrubs in the 'Australian Alps'. The climate here is challenging for a small mammal: cold and wet, with frequent snowfalls and strong winds.

Its range is restricted to just three isolated populations in southeast Australia: Kosciuszko National Park in New South Wales; and in Victoria the Mt Bogong–Mt Higginbotham range and Mt Buller-Stirling areas.

Personal pantry

Unlike many of its close relatives, this possum is not a tree-dweller, but it can move around nimbly in the low shrubs that are dotted around the hillsides of its mountain home. It is nocturnal and spends the day curled up in a ball to keep warm. Evidence from captivity suggests that individuals may huddle together for extra warmth. Females occupy communal nesting sites and have overlapping home ranges. Males are nomadic and associate with females only to breed.

Changing seasons call for changing diets. During summer the mountain pygmy possum feeds on energy-rich foods such as moths, which migrate into the area to breed, as well as other arthropods including caterpillars, beetles and spiders. As winter approaches it switches to seeds and berries.

When winter really sets in, during May–September, this species goes to sleep and hibernates, surviving off fat reserves stored up during times of plenty. It is the only Australian mammal to do this. Occasionally it also wakes up to eat seeds and berries hoarded in its own larder.

WHERE TO SEE IT

The two largest populations occur in Victoria, near Mt Blue Cow and Charlotte Pass ski resorts at Mt Hotham, Falls Creek and Mt Buller. In New South Wales pygmy possums also inhabit a tiny area within Kosiuszko National Park. Look out on late afternoons in summer as they hunt moths among the boulder fields.

THREATS

The highly restricted habitat of this species is threatened by rock extraction, and by the development of infrastructure for recreational skiing. It also falls victim frequently to introduced predators such as foxes and cats.

28
EDGE RANK

Leadbeater's possum

Gymnobelideus leadbeateri

Head/body length: 150–170mm
Tail length: 150–180mm; Weight: 110–165g

WHERE TO SEE IT

Leadbeater's possum has been recorded in Yarra Ranges and Baw Baw National Parks, and Lake Mountain State Park. A small population also survives at Yellingbo Nature Conservation Reserve, 50km east of Melbourne. Numerous volunteer-based research projects focus on this species. You could help 'stag watch' – literally sit under a tree in the evening and record any emerging possums: www.earthwatch.org/site/pp2.asp?c=crLQK3PHLsF&b=1322207. More details at: http://cres.anu.edu.au/dbl/friendsoflbp.php

THREATS

This species depends heavily on old mountain ash trees for nest sites. These trees are threatened by logging and uncontrolled wild fires.

54
EDGE RANK

Fear of flying?

Leadbeater's possum belongs to a group called marsupial gliders, which have evolved a lifestyle similar to flying squirrels: rather than running up and down trees, they glide between them, using flaps of skin between their front and back legs.

This species differs from the others in one crucial respect: it doesn't have a gliding membrane! It does, however, have a long bushy tail, large ears and eyes, and thick soft fur. Its grey-brown coat has a dark stripe running from the top of the head and down the spine. There are also dark patches around the ears and eyes and its club-shaped tail is broader at the tip than the base.

From the ashes

Leadbeater's possum is very selective when it comes to its habitat requirements. It can survive only in regenerating or mixed-age ash forests that contain both eucalyptus species and old hollow mountain ash trees.

Thought to be extinct after disastrous fires in 1939, it was rediscovered in 1961 in Marysville near Melbourne, Australia. Today it is known from a range of no more than 3,500 km² at the western end of Victoria's Central Highlands, at elevations of 500–1,500m, with another small population just east of Melbourne.

Girl power

This species is nocturnal and monogamous. The female is dominant, and vigorously defends her small territory (1–3ha) against other mature females, including her own daughters. Within each territory a single nest is made inside a hollow mountain ash tree. This can house a small colony of two to ten animals, comprising the reproducing pair, their offspring and unrelated mature males. Nest mates share in mutual grooming and recognise one another through smell.

Breeding occurs year-round with pregnancy lasting no more than 20 days. Following birth, the underdeveloped young crawl into their mother's pouch for protection and milk, where they remain until big enough to venture out. Females are weaned at ten months; males at 15 months.

The diet consists mainly of insects and spiders taken from behind the bark of eucalyptus trees.

The possums also cut notches in acacia bark with their teeth and feed on the oozing gum.

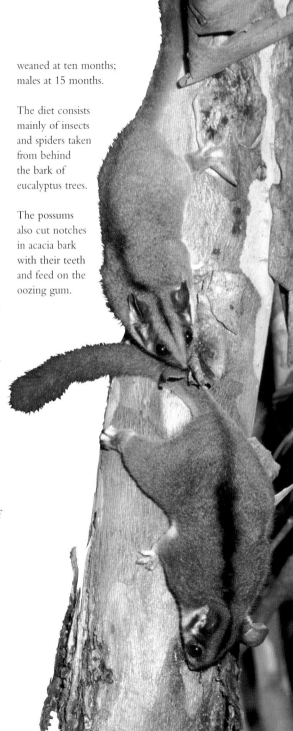

New Zealand lesser short-tailed bat

Mystacina tuberculata

Head/body length: 60–80mm
Forearm length: 40–45mm
Tail length: 10–12mm; Weight: 25–35g

Bat walk

Bats are the only mammals that can truly fly, yet this species lives a life much like mice or shrews. It is the most terrestrial bat in the world, more at home on the ground than flying through the air.

The lesser short-tailed bat has large ears and a short muzzle. Its fur is grey-brown above and paler below. When the wings are not in use for flying the forearms are folded to act as front legs for walking and climbing. The thumb has a large claw and the back feet have talons, both to help the bat clamber around easily.

This species is both endemic to New Zealand and the country's last remaining native terrestrial mammal. It is found on both the North and South Islands as well as some outlying islands, inhabiting heavily forested areas with native trees such as totara, kauri and beech. Scientists think it may be the sole survivor of an ancient lineage; its cousin, the greater short-tailed bat, was last seen in 1967 and is now believed to be extinct.

Floor plan

Scientists know very little about this most atypical bat. Small groups roost in hollow trees and caves, and it is possible they use their teeth and claws to excavate roosting holes in rotten wood. Remarkably agile on the ground, they spend large amounts of time of the forest floor, feeding on insects, fruit, nectar and pollen. Food is located with a combination of echolocation, smell and sound. This species is thought to be an important plant pollinator.

WHERE TO SEE IT

Probably easiest to find on North Island, where a total population of about 40,000 bats is divided between sites at Rangataua, Pureora, Kaimanawa, Whirinaki, Urewera, Waitaanga and Waitotara. Other known populations are on Little Barrier Island in the Hauraki Gulf, on Codfish Island (offshore from Stewart Island) and in Kahurangi National Park. In an ambitious conservation project, pregnant females from a 300-strong colony in Tararua Forest Park were captured in December 2004 and taken to Pukaha Mount National Wildlife Centre, where they gave birth to 20 pups. These have since been translocated to Kapiti Island in an attempt to establish an 'insurance population' in a predator-free environment. Visits to Kapiti are restricted to fifty people per day and a landing permit must be obtained in advance.
Details at: www.kapiti.org.nz/kapiti.html

THREATS

The lesser short-tailed bat is threatened by destruction of native forests: 66% of New Zealand's lowland forest has been cleared to make way for development, farming and timber extraction. Having evolved without ground predators, it is also vulnerable to introduced species like rats and cats, which have devastated populations of many native New Zealand species.

=56
EDGE RANK

Proserpine rock wallaby

Petrogale persephone

Head/body length: approx. 60–65cm
Tail length: approx 60–70cm
Weight: 6.4–8.8kg

WHERE TO SEE IT

This sure-footed rock-hopper can be found in small colonies around the town of Airlie Beach. It also occurs in Conway, Dryander and Gloucester Island National Parks.

Queensland

THREATS

This is the only rock wallaby considered threatened. It inhabits areas with high human pressure and may also lose out in competition with other species of rock wallaby. In 1997, 26 colonies were known, with 14 on private land and the rest in national parks and state forests.

336
EDGE RANK

Getting a grip

Rock wallabies have the distinctive shape of a typical kangaroo or wallaby, and are essentially smaller versions of their better-known cousins. The Proserpine rock wallaby is grey to brown in colour, with pale flecks on the fur. It also has a pale grey band running from the corner of the mouth to the ears and a distinctive white tip to its tail. It is larger and longer tailed than most rock wallabies.

This species inhabits boulder outcrops, where its padded soles give it a good grip on the rough surface. It lives among semi-deciduous vine and acacia forests, and is a relic of a wetter time when rainforest covered much greater areas of Australia. Discovered only in 1977 near the town of Proserpine, it has a very restricted range in Whitsunday Shire in Queensland. This encompasses the Clarke Range near Proserpine, and the northern, eastern and parts of the western margins of the Conway Range.

Good breeding

Little is known about the specific habits of this rock wallaby. It is timid and rarely ventures far from the shelter of the rocky outcrops and forest where it lives. When alarmed it even climbs trees. It eats mainly broad leaves, but during dry spells will move to the forest edge to graze grasses. Home ranges are thought to be around 30 hectares.

The life of a rock wallaby seems to revolve around producing young. Its gestation period is 33–34 days, and amazingly females mate again within hours of a birth. Youngsters develop in their mother's pouch for around 210 days before taking their own steps into the world. And generally the day one infant exits, the next one is born.

Conserving wildlife in Australasia

Australasia, comprising the islands of Australia, New Zealand, New Guinea and Melanesia, has long been geographically separated from the other great landmasses of the world. This has allowed many unique species to evolve: in Australia alone, 83% of the 360 or so mammals are found nowhere else on Earth. Unfortunately this very isolation has left the region's wildlife highly vulnerable to outside interference, and the late arrival of our species on the scene proved little short of catastrophic for many native animals. This problem intensified with the advent of European settlement in 1788, since when 27 mammal species have already become extinct.

Alien nation

European settlers brought a mixed bag of species from their homelands to Australasia, many of which have since wreaked havoc on native species. In Australia the most notorious villains are red foxes, feral cats, rabbits and cane toads. The foxes are devastating predators of small and medium-sized mammals, whose evolution had not equipped them to outwit such a foe; the rabbits out-compete native ground-dwelling herbivores (and sustain the large fox and feral cat populations); and the toads not only eat small animals but are lethally toxic to larger animals, such as quolls, that attempt to eat them. The Australian government is involved in a number of schemes to reduce the populations of these and other introduced species. One such scheme, Stop the Toad (*www.stopthetoad.org.au*), is working hard to prevent the cane toad population from spreading into Western Australia: its activities include an annual 'toad muster' where volunteers eradicate as many toads as they can at the Timber Creek buffer zone.

The smaller the island, the more harm invasive alien species are likely to do to native wildlife. New Zealand's remarkable native fauna included few predators, so the arrival of the Maori, who hunted the nine species of flightless moa to extinction, and then European settlers, who brought with them predators like rats, cats and stoats, was devastating. Today, recovery plans for the endangered lesser short-tailed bat and flightless birds like the kakapo, a rare ground-dwelling parrot, include maintaining populations on offshore islands from which alien predators have been eradicated. Forest and Bird (*www.forestandbird.org.nz*), New Zealand's leading conservation organisation, sponsors recovery programmes for the bats, as well as kakapos, kiwis, takahes and other threatened native species.

Chipping away

During the 1960–70s a woodchipping industry became established in Australia, whereby large tracts of old-growth native forest were clear-felled and the wood chipped for use in the manufacture of low-grade paper and chipboard.

▲ **Dead parrot walking:** Thought extinct in 1970, New Zealand's flightless kakapo is now the subject of a successful relocation programme.

▼ **Forest secrets:** In 2005, New Guinea's Foja mountains revealed a new population of golden-mantled tree kangaroo.

▲ **Hopping mad:** The introduction of cane toads to Australia has spelled disaster for many native species.

Untapped potential

▲ **Breaking down barriers:** Global warming threatens the Great Barrier Reef and its unique ecosystems.

▲ **Wildfire:** Drought is making Australia's arid south even more prone to destructive bush fires.

This low-cost, high-volume commodity plays a significant role in Australia's economy and, despite strong and growing public opposition to the practice, the industry still operates today in Tasmania, Western Australia and elsewhere. One organisation dedicated to ending the destruction of old-growth forest is the Western Australian Forest Alliance (*www.wafa.org.au*) which lobbies the government and raises public awareness of the issue. The state government's latest Forest Management plan, spanning 2004–13, promises increased protection for and better management of Western Australia's old-growth forest, and has been broadly welcomed by WAFA.

Loss of forest and the associated release of carbon is one of the key causes of global warming, and Australia is likely to prove especially vulnerable to the damaging consequences of climate change. Projections suggest that the arid south of the country will become even drier, increasing the risk of drought and bushfires, while the country's long coastline is at risk of inundation as sea levels rise. An increase in sea temperature could do massive damage to one of Australia's most important natural and economic assets, the Great Barrier Reef, while land animals are likely to suffer

massive habitat degradation and loss. The Big Switch (*www.thebigswitch.org.au*) is a national campaign from a large coalition of organisations, businesses and community groups that seeks to raise awareness of how ordinary Australians can take action to combat climate change.

Australia's indigenous people have long respected the country's native wildlife, which is deeply enshrined in their culture. Today, the burgeoning support for conservation movements suggests that the wider human population of Australasia is beginning to share that view. But time is short.

Africa

The very word Africa conjures up images of teeming herds on endless plains where lions and other predators lurk in deadly ambush. Many of the animals that inhabit these areas – from outlandish giraffes and zebras to lumbering elephants and rhinos – need no introduction: whether as cuddly toys, cartoon characters or stars of our favourite television dramas, they have embedded themselves in our culture.

But this picture-book scenario represents only a fraction of what Africa has to offer. Elsewhere there is also the world's biggest desert, its second-largest tropical rainforest and its highest free-standing mountain. These less publicised places are home to all manner of creatures, many virtually unknown, but no less interesting or important. How many people have heard of an addax, a bonobo or an otter-shrew?

It is ironic that Africa, the cradle of humanity, should be one of the last areas our own species thoroughly explored. It is also heartening, in the age of mobile phones and globalisation, that there are parts we have yet to reach. Nonetheless, the relentless plundering of the continent's resources and the continued expansion of its human population now leave many of its wild animals struggling for survival.

 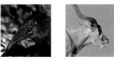

◀ *The cheetah is the supreme hunter of Africa's open savannahs. This female is stalking gazelles in Serengeti National Park, Tanzania.*

0 500 km 1000 km 1500 km

0 500 1000 miles

Tunisia

Morocco

Western Sahara

Algeria

Libya

Egypt

River Nile

Mauritania

Mali

Niger

Chad

Sudan

Eritrea

Djibouti

Senegal

The Gambia

Guinea Bissau

Guinea

Sierra Leone

Liberia

Ivory Coast

Burkina

Ghana

Togo

Benin

River Niger

Nigeria

Cameroon

Central African Republic

Ethiopia

Somalia

Somali Peninsula

Uganda

Kenya

Equatorial Guinea

Gabon

Congo

Congo Basin

River Congo

Democratic Republic of the Congo

Rwanda

Burundi

Lake Victoria

Mt. Kilimanjaro

Tanzania

Angola

Zambia

Zambezi

Malawi

Mozambique

Namib Desert

Namibia

Zimbabwe

Botswana

Kalahari

South Africa

Lesotho

Swaziland

Addax
p92
The Sahara: scattered from Chad to Mauritania

African wild ass
p79
Horn of Africa: Somalia, Ethiopia and Eritrea

Mountain nyala
p93
Bale Mountains, Ethiopia

Grevy's zebra
p83
Northern Kenya; possibly Ethiopia

Hirola
p93
Western Kenya; possibly Somalia

Golden-rumped elephant shrew
p82
Western Kenya

Mountain gorilla
p94
Virunga Mountains: Uganda, Rwanda, DRC

Black rhinoceros
p80
Sub-Saharan Africa: scattered from South Africa to Kenya

Pygmy hippopotamus
p77
West Africa: Liberia to Niger Delta

Nimba otter-shrew
p82
Côte D'Ivoire and Liberia

Bonobo
p84
Congo River Basin, DRC

African wild dog
p86
Southern and eastern Africa: widespread but scattered

Cheetah
p87
Southern and eastern Africa: widespread but scattered

African elephant
p90
Sub-Saharan Africa, mostly in protected areas

Riverine rabbit
p78
Karoo plateau, South Africa

Mediterranean scrub

Semidesert

Desert

Wetland

Steppe (grass, brush and thicket)

Savanna

Woodland savanna

Tropical rainforest

Temperate and montane grassland

Mountains

East African coastal forest

Pygmy hippopotamus

Hexaprotodon liberiensis

Head/body length: 150–175cm
Height at shoulder: 70–90cm
Tail length: 15–20cm; Weight: 180–275kg

WHERE TO SEE IT

Walking safaris in Liberia's Sapo National Park occasionally provide a rare encounter. This park is probably home to the largest remaining pygmy hippo population. The area has suffered through years of civil unrest, but rebuilding work is now under way. For details, contact the Society for the Conservation of Nature of Liberia (SCNL) (*email: scnlib2001@yahoo.com*). Alternatively try Tai National Park in Côte d'Ivoire from December to February.

THREATS

The rainforests of West Africa are already severely fragmented, and logging – together with the advance of farming and human settlements – is reducing them still further. Deforestation is especially rampant In Liberia, the pygmy hippo's last stronghold. As remote forests become more accessible, the hippos become increasingly vulnerable to hunting for the bushmeat trade.

21
EDGE RANK

Half-pint hippo

Imagine a hippo that has shrunk in the wash. This Lilliputian version of its bigger and better-known cousin has a barrel-like body, short stocky legs and smooth, greenish-black skin. Besides its size, it differs from the common hippo in having a more rounded head, with eyes set on the side rather than protruding from the top, and separate toes rather than webbed feet. Its short muzzle houses tusk-like incisors and canines that grow rapidly to become formidable weapons.

Like a common hippo, the pygmy version has a number of special adaptations to its semi-aquatic existence, including ears and nostrils that it can close when submerged. It also secretes a thick, oily, pinkish-white substance known as 'blood-sweat' from pores in its skin. This both allows it to stay longer under water and protects it from drying out when exposed to warm air.

River horse

The name hippopotamus translates as 'river horse' in ancient Greek. And, just like its larger cousin, this animal spends long periods resting in rivers or swamps. However, the ranges of the two species do not overlap. The pygmy hippo is confined to the dense lowland rainforests of West Africa, with small population pockets in Liberia, Sierra Leone, Guinea and Côte d'Ivoire, and a few very isolated groups in Nigeria's Niger Delta. A 1993 estimate suggested that just 2,000–3,000 animals remain. This number has almost certainly fallen since then.

Muck spreader

Pygmy hippos lose water easily through their delicate skin, so they spend the heat of the day resting and wallowing in swamps or hollows along the sides of streams. When it gets cooler during the late afternoon, they emerge to begin feeding along a labyrinth of trails that they create by 'tunnelling' through the thick vegetation. They are strict vegetarians, eating grasses, shoots and fallen fruits and continue foraging through the night.

Unlike their larger cousins, pygmy hippos avoid a crowd. Males and females meet only briefly in order to mate. The rest of the time they are antisocial – and in more ways than one, reinforcing their territorial boundaries by scattering their sloppy droppings far and wide with a vigorous tail wagging as they wander their trails.

Riverine rabbit

Bunolagus monticularis

Head/body length: 340–470 mm
Tail length: 70–110 mm
Ear length: 110–125 mm
Weight: 1.5kg (males); 1.8kg (females)

WHERE TO SEE IT

This requires careful planning and consultation, as all surviving rabbits live on privately owned land. Conservation efforts are co-ordinated by the Riverine Rabbit Conservation Project, which is encouraging farmers to be more sympathetic to the rabbit's requirements. To date, three Riverine Rabbit Conservancies have been established in the Karoo: one in the Northern Cape and two in the Western Cape. Additionally, several farmers have declared their farms Natural Heritage Sites to protect the rabbit and its habitat. Anyone wanting to see this species *must* contact the Riverine Rabbit Conservation Project in advance: www.riverinerabbit.co.za

THREATS

Dramatic habitat loss through the advance of wheat cultivation has devastated the population. Continued pressure from farms still threatens those rabbits that survive, as do hunting, trapping, feral cats and dogs, and further loss of riverside habitat through the building of dams.

3
EDGE RANK

Big-eared bunny

It is instantly obvious that hearing is very important to this animal, as it sports enormous radar-dish ears. Otherwise it looks similar in size and shape to your average bunny rabbit. Its fur is light brown above, including its woolly tail, with a cream-coloured belly and throat. A distinctive dark brown stripe runs across the cheek towards the base of the ear, and it has a white ring around the eye.

Soil survival

This species is endemic to South Africa, where it is restricted to a single river system in the central region of the Karoo Plateau in Cape Province. Here it inhabits dense thickets and similar salt-tolerant vegetation that grows along the banks of seasonal rivers. It is highly dependent on areas with the kind of fine, sandy soil that is suitable for excavating burrows.

Over the past 70 years the population has slumped by at least 60% and today perhaps fewer than 250 mature individuals survive. These are scattered across a number of fragmented subpopulations, none of which contains more than 50 animals.

Slow progress

By day riverine rabbits tuck themselves away under bushes and sleep in a shallow scrape in the soil, called a form. They become active after dark, when they awake to browse on riverside vegetation. Their diet consists mostly of flowers and leaves, though this may also extend to grass – especially in the wet season.

This species is solitary. Males and females each have separate home ranges, with male ranges overlapping those of the females. Unfortunately though, when it comes to reproduction, this is one bunny that doesn't breed like proverbial rabbits. Females have just one or two young each year, and so, with

longevity seldom more than three years, each produces only around four offspring during her lifetime. This makes riverine rabbits extremely vulnerable and dramatically reduces the likelihood of their population recovering naturally.

African wild ass
Equus africanus

Head/body length: 200 cm; Height at shoulder: 125cm
Tail length: 45cm; Weight: 250kg

WHERE TO SEE IT

The Messir Plateau in Eritrea's Asaila Mountains has recently become a reserve for the African wild ass, and protects over 400. Wild asses also occur in Ethiopia's Yangudi-Rassa National Park and Mille-Serdo Wild Ass Reserve, but they must share these areas with livestock. Israel's Yotvata Hai-Bar Nature Reserve protects an introduced population, outside their natural range, and aims to establish breeding and reintroduction programmes.

THREATS

The species was domesticated about 6,000 years ago. Today donkeys are found worldwide, but only a handful of their wild ancestors survive. Uncontrolled hunting for meat and body parts has devastated wild populations, and in Ethiopia and Somalia this has been exacerbated by ongoing political instability. Meanwhile the spread of farming and domestic livestock has driven wild asses from their traditional food and water sources, while interbreeding with donkeys has undermined their genetic integrity.

13
EDGE RANK

Ancestral ass

This species is easily recognisable as being the ancestor of domestic donkeys, with its stocky body, big head, stiff mane and unmistakable long ears. Its coat is light grey to reddish brown above and white below, sometimes with a dark stripe along the spine or dark bands around the legs. Long, narrow hooves give it amazing surefootedness.

Some like it hot

Few would choose to live in the hottest, driest places on earth, but that's just where the African wild ass thrives. Hot spots, so to speak, include stony deserts, arid bushland and dry grasslands – though not sand dunes. It mostly stays within 30km of water, since it must drink at least every three days.

This species once occurred right across North Africa and possibly into Arabia. It is even mentioned in the Bible. Today, however, the 570 or so that remain are confined to the Horn of Africa, with 400 in Eritrea, fewer than 160 in Ethiopia and about ten in Somalia. A separate, larger population in Sudan probably comprises feral descendants of domestic donkeys.

Thirst quencher

Tough terrain produces tough animals and the African wild ass is no exception. Among its desert survival adaptations is the capacity to lose up to 30% of its body weight in water, and then restore this in just five minutes of drinking. Like all horses it is a grazer, preferring grasses, where available. It moves and feeds in the cool of the early morning and late afternoon, spending the hot hours resting in the shade – usually in hilly areas.

With food in the desert thin on the ground, African wild asses live in small family groups of no more than ten. These may stay together for several weeks, depending on resources. Stallions are loners, and may take up territories around water sources in order to secure mates. Females become sexually mature at three to four years, giving birth to a single foal during the wet season.

Black rhinoceros

Diceros bicornis

Head/body length: 300–375 cm
Height at shoulder: 140–170cm; Tail length: 60–70cm
Horn length: up to 80cm; Weight: 800–1400kg

WHERE TO SEE IT

Some of Africa's most famous parks still harbour this relic from the earliest days of mammals. Tanzania's Ngorongoro Crater offers reliable sightings, as does Kenya's Nairobi National Park. Namibia's Damaraland region and Etosha National Park are amongst the best places in southern Africa, along with South Africa's Hluhluwe, Imfolozi and Mkhuzi game reserves.

THREATS

This animal has been long and heavily persecuted, at first for sport and then for profit. The population plummeted from the turn of the 20th century to 65,000 by the 1970s. An increased demand for rhino horn – primarily to make Arabian dagger handles, but also for traditional Oriental medicine – saw it become more valuable than gold, precipitating a further dramatic decline to just 2,400. After some conservation successes numbers are now slowly rising.

7
EDGE RANK

Black or white?

So are black rhinos really black? Well no, they are actually pale brown or grey. African rhino names come not from their colours, but rather the shape of their mouths. The term 'white' is a corruption of the word 'wide', referring to a white rhino's broad, square-lipped mouth. Black rhinos were so named to prevent confusion. Obvious really!

Putting colour aside, the black rhino is about half the size of its white cousin and has a distinctive, prehensile upper lip, which protrudes beyond its lower lip. In common with white rhinos, it also has two horns, the front generally being the thinner and longer. These are made from keratin, a protein found in human hair and nails.

Beating about the bush

This versatile rhino is at home in many habitats, from semi-desert and grassland to dense bush and woodland, but prefers areas with plenty of bushes, which provide both food and shelter. It once roamed throughout sub-Saharan Africa, wherever habitat was suitable. Today, however, it is largely confined to reserves in South Africa, Namibia, Zimbabwe, Tanzania and Kenya, with a total population estimated at around 3,725.

Scientists recognise four separate subspecies. The most endangered is the western black rhino, which was last recorded in northern Cameroon but may now be extinct. The eastern black rhino's stronghold is Kenya, where there are perhaps 540 animals, with a further 60 or so

in neighbouring Tanzania. The south-western subspecies numbers around 1,140 in Namibia, with another 80 in South Africa. The south-central black rhino is the most numerous, with around 1,866 animals, mainly in South Africa and with smaller numbers in Zimbabwe and southern Tanzania. It has also been successfully reintroduced to Swaziland, Zambia, Botswana and Malawi.

Just browsing

Its hooked lip reveals that the black rhino, unlike its larger, grazing cousin, is a specialist browser. It uses this appendage to select favourite morsels from over 200 different species of plant, plucking leaves, twigs, herbs and legumes with surprising delicacy. Succulent plants also provide much of its water intake, so it can go four or five days without drinking. Most feeding takes place in early morning, late afternoon or after dark. During the heat of the day waterholes or mud wallows provide a much cooler alternative.

Black rhinos have excellent hearing and a very good sense of smell. But their poor eyesight means they are quick to become agitated, hence their notoriously grumpy reputation. Despite the one-tonne bulk, this animal is alarmingly agile and speedy: at full tilt it can top 50km/h and would easily outrun an Olympic sprinter.

Apart from cows with young calves, black rhinos are generally solitary – though small groups sometimes gather at wallows and salt licks. Males are strictly territorial, while females often have overlapping home ranges. They become fully mature at around seven years, and give birth every two to five years. In the wild black rhinos may reach the ripe old age of 30–35.

Golden-rumped elephant-shrew

Rhynchocyon chrysopygus

Head/body length: 230–280mm
Tail length: 210–240mm
Weight: around 540g

Flexible friend

Looking like an alien extra from *Star Wars*, this extraordinary creature has a flexible, trunk-like nose and a bright yellow backside. It also has large eyes and ears, stick-thin legs, and a long, rat-like tail. A thick patch of skin on the male's rump, called a 'dermal shield', helps protect it from the biting attacks of rivals.

Today this elephant-shrew is confined to a few coastal forest patches in Kenya. Notably Arabuko-Sokoke Forest, with an estimated population of 10,000–20,000.

'Til death us do part

The golden-rumped elephant shrew is strictly monogamous: pairs stick together until one partner dies. The two spend little time in one another's company, however, simply keeping in touch via scent marking. They forage by day, using their snout to root through leaf litter for earthworms and other invertebrates. At night they sleep in a nest of dry leaves on the forest floor.

Females produce up to six young per year, with each one born singly after around 40 days' gestation. Infants are weaned after around two weeks in the nest.

WHERE TO SEE IT

Try the Arabuko-Sokoke forest on the Kenyan coast road. Pick up a guidebook and guide at the visitor centre, then follow one of the well-marked trails. Early morning or late afternoon is best. Details at: www.assets-kenya.org/asf.htm

THREATS

Habitat destruction is the main threat, with suitable forest in short supply and shrinking fast. Arabuko-Sokoke is under threat from encroaching agriculture and woodcarvers who fell trees to fashion tourist curios.

46 EDGE RANK

Nimba otter-shrew

Micropotamogale lamottei

Head/body length: 120–55 mm
Tail length: approx. 95–135 mm; Weight: approx. 60–95g

Water repellent

A brief glimpse of this animal swimming, with its long tail streaming out behind, suggests a rat or

water vole. However it is related to neither, belonging instead to an ancient group of animals that have more in common with the aquatic tenrec of Madagascar (see page 114). Its soft, grey-brown, water-repellent fur is a natty adaptation to its watery lifestyle – although, surprisingly, it lacks the flattened tail or webbed feet of the tenrec.

River deep, mountain high

The Nimba otter-shrew lives in upland forest streams and swampy areas. It is restricted to an area of less than 1,500 km², centred on Mount Nimba on the border of Côte d'Ivoire and Guinea, and the Putu mountain range in Liberia.

Touch sensitive

We know very little about this endearing creature. It is solitary, sleeps in burrows by day, and uses its stiff, sensitive whiskers to hunt for crustaceans, small fish and tadpoles along the stream bed.

WHERE TO SEE IT

Rather a difficult proposition: Mount Nimba at the heart of the otter-shrew's range is a restricted area, and only scientists with permission from the authorities are authorised to visit.

THREATS

Mining activities have devastated large areas of suitable habitat. It is also sometimes accidentally caught and drowned in fish traps.

55 EDGE RANK

Grevy's zebra

Equus grevyi

Head/body length: 250–300cm
Shoulder height: 140–160cm
Tail length: 38–60cm; Weight: 350–450kg

Changes of stripes

This handsome animal looks rather different from the familiar plains zebra of most wildlife documentaries. First, it is much larger – being the largest living wild horse. Second, it sports a pattern of very narrow stripes, like a pinstripe suit. And third, it has large dish-like ears, with which it signals to its companions.

All zebras are white with black stripes. In Grevy's zebra, however, the stripes do not extend onto its belly and inner thighs, which are plain white. Furthermore, unlike other zebras, its stripes become even narrower towards its hindquarters. The mane is stiff and striped and, in foals, extends right along the back to the base of the tail.

Habitat sandwich

Grevy's zebra has evolved to live in the semi-deserts and arid grasslands that stretch from northern Kenya across Somalia and Ethiopia to the Eritrean coast. This habitat niche is sandwiched between those of its two relatives: the African wild ass, which inhabits more arid areas to the north; and the plains zebra, which inhabits wetter regions to the south.

Its distribution once mirrored its habitat. Today, however, it is largely restricted to northern Kenya, with perhaps an isolated few just clinging on in Ethiopia. The total wild population has declined by 75% since the 1970s. Only around 3,000 remain.

Social misfit

Unlike its cousins, Grevy's zebra is not particularly sociable. A mare with her latest foal or foals makes up the basic unit. Sometimes these units come together, but no-one takes charge and the group may split up at any time. Larger herds sometimes form during times of migration or drought.

Males may form small bachelor herds. Breeding stallions become territorial and defend large areas to get exclusive access to any passing females on heat. These territories measure up to 12km² and are among the largest known for any herbivore. Mating occurs throughout the year. A single foal is born after a gestation period of around 390 days and remains with its mother for up to three years.

WHERE TO SEE IT

You can see Grevy's zebra quite easily in Kenya's Samburu and Buffalo Springs reserves, and in the private reserves of the Laikipia Plateau, on the lower northern slopes of Mount Kenya.

THREATS

The beautiful coat of this species has been its downfall, with hunting – partly fuelled by the fashion markets of Europe and North America – causing its drastic decline. Although the skin trade all but ended in 1979 when hunting was declared illegal, people in remote areas still kill Grevy's zebras for their meat. Today habitat loss and degradation, primarily from overgrazing by livestock, poses a further threat.

=82
EDGE RANK

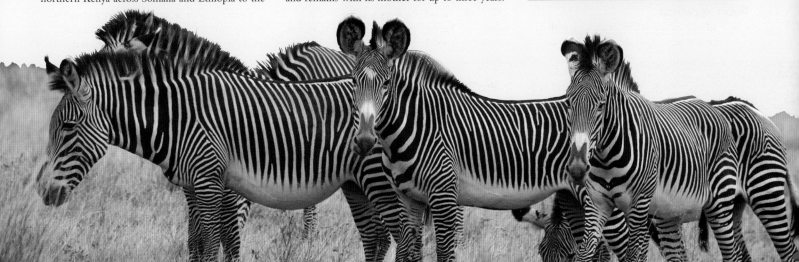

Bonobo

Pan paniscus

Height when upright: 90–100cm
Head/body length: 55–60cm
Weight: 30–35kg (males); 25–30kg (females)

Elegant ape

The bonobo was the last of the great apes to be
discovered and, together with the chimpanzee, it is
our closest living relative. Amazingly, we share over
95% of our genetic make-up with this animal.
Although similar in size to the better-known
chimp, it is sometimes known as the 'pygmy
chimpanzee' due to its more slender and elegant
build – an impression that is emphasized by the
sleek fur that covers its long limbs.

Like a chimp, a bonobo's coat is jet black and
sometimes turns grey with age. Unlike chimps,
however, its face is also black. The flattened hair on
its scalp sticks out sideways, as though arranged in
a central parting, and it is less liable to baldness
than chimps.

Bonobos live in a mosaic of humid primary and
secondary lowland rainforest and swamp. They are
found only in the Democratic Republic of Congo
in central Africa, inhabiting a low-lying basin
enclosed between the River Zaire, the River
Sankuru-Kasai and the River Lualaba.

Make love, not war

How often do you think about sex? We're told that
men think about it a lot more than women. Well,
not if you're a bonobo. These are highly intelligent,
social animals and sex is central to their society. The
power of female seduction has taken over the need
for male dominance. Individuals in a group have
regular 'quickies' to reinforce bonds, and these can
be between members of the opposite or same sex.

During disputes, sex involving all combinations
of age, sex and status helps to defuse the situation.
Mutual masturbation is common in females, and
both homo- and heterosexual couples have sex
face-to-face – highly unusual behaviour among
non-human primates.

Bonobos live in stable communities that may
contain up to 150 members, although these usually
split into smaller groups to travel and find food.
They spend most of their time in trees looking for
fruit, but also eat smaller amounts of stems, leaves
and occasionally invertebrates. Unlike chimps, they
do not hunt other animals. When the necessity
arises, they will travel on the ground by 'knuckle
walking'. They build tree nests of twigs and leaves
in which to sleep.

Courtship is gentler and more tentative, but more
frequent than in any other primate. Swellings on a
female's rump advertise when she is ready to mate,
but there is no specific breeding season. She gives
birth to a single baby after eight months' gestation,
and cares for it for nearly five years.

WHERE TO SEE IT

This may well be the first great ape to become extinct. In recent years its entire range has been blighted by civil war in the Democratic Republic of Congo. Previously most research took place in Wamba Forest, but many bonobos in the area have since been killed. The population at the Lomako study site fared better and returning scientists are now seeing bonobos again. You can also encounter bonobos at Lui Kotal, at the very southwestern tip of Salonga National Park, south of the Lokoro River. Details at: www.bonobo.org/fieldsites.html; www.panafricanprimates.org/lola_ya_bonobo.htm; www.friendsofbonobos.org

THREATS

Bonobos are not as widespread as their chimpanzee cousins, so any threats to their survival are that much more acute. Loss of habitat inevitably takes its toll, as large areas of rainforest are cleared for agriculture, timber extraction and development. Strong local beliefs have traditionally prevented local people from hunting and eating bonobos, but the massive proliferation of the bushmeat trade has changed this and hunting for the pot is now a serious concern. All these threats are exacerbated by ongoing political instability in the region.

237
EDGE RANK

Democratic Republic of Congo

African wild dog
Lycaon pictus

Head/body length: 75–110; Height at shoulder: 60–75cm
Tail length: 30–40cm; Weight: 20–35kg

WHERE TO SEE IT

Because wild dogs roam over such vast areas, finding them is difficult. It is easiest when they are denning and their movements are more predictable. Top spots include Selous, Mikumi and Ruaha reserves in Tanzania, Moremi Game Reserve in Botswana, and Kruger National Park in South Africa.

THREATS

Wild dogs require lots of space and their swift decline is due mainly to habitat fragmentation. As good habitats shrink, they are forced into more competition with other large carnivores, notably lions and spotted hyenas. Wild dogs have an undeserved reputation for attacking livestock, and are therefore persecuted mercilessly. Road accidents and incidental snaring have also become serious threats – as has disease carried by domestic dogs, such as canine distemper and rabies, to which wild dogs' sociable habits make them particularly vulnerable.

No ranking
EDGE RANK

Painted pooch

This dog has a distinctive combination of lean, leggy build and beautiful coat, with each individual sporting its own unique 'painted' pattern of yellow, grey, black and white blotches. Other striking features include a bushy tail and big 'Mickey Mouse' ears, with which to tune in to the distant calls of companions.

Dog gone

Wild dogs thrive in any open country with enough prey, from plains and semi-desert to bushy savannah, woodlands and upland forest. They have even been seen near the summit of Mount Kilimanjaro. Unfortunately, however, their range has shrunk more dramatically than that of any other African carnivore. Once widespread across sub-Saharan Africa, wild dogs now occur only in scattered populations in southern and eastern Africa, the most stable being in Botswana, Zimbabwe, Zambia, South Africa and Tanzania.

Co-operative killer

Wild dogs are out-and-out meat eaters. They hunt in co-operative packs, generally targeting medium-sized antelopes such as impala, but are also able to take beasts as large as wildebeest. The pack wears down its prey in a sustained high-speed chase and, as it tires, they close in and tear at its rear, flanks and legs. Once downed, the prey is killed and consumed with great speed and efficiency.

This species lives in packs, like many wild canines, but its social system is unusual in that just one dominant pair breeds, while all other pack members help look after the pups – even bringing back and regurgitating food to them after hunting forays. Packs can number 20 or more, with new packs forming when subgroups disperse and join up with unrelated subgroups elsewhere. Outside the breeding season, wild dogs wander far and wide in search of prey; home ranges can be as large as 2,000 km², but may be restricted to much less.

The average litter size of ten is the largest of any dog species. Puppies are born blind and helpless in dens, and remain inside for around three months, while all pack members help look after them. They reach independence at 16–24 months, but few wild dogs survive beyond ten years.

Cheetah

Acinonyx jubatus

Head/body length: 110–150cm
Height at shoulder: 70–90cm
Tail length: 65–90cm
Weight: 35–65kg

WHERE TO SEE IT

In East Africa the grassy plains of the Serengeti and Maasai Mara are perfect cheetah country, with Kenya's Amboseli also being good. Further south, Namibia's Etosha National Park, Botswana's Moremi, and South Africa's Kruger National Park and Kgalagadi Transfrontier Park all produce reliable sightings. Make sure your vehicle does not disturb a cheetah while hunting.

THREATS

An extraordinary lack of genetic diversity among today's cheetahs suggests that the entire population passed through a severe genetic bottleneck at some point in its evolutionary history – probably during an ice age. All living cheetahs may even be descended from a single female. This makes them particularly vulnerable to disease. In some areas, notably Namibia, conflict with livestock farmers also remains a problem.

299
EDGE RANK

Catwalk model

The cheetah is a greyhound in cat's clothing. Everything about its appearance – the light frame, long limbs, and sleek, streamlined body – says 'built for speed'. And a top speed of up to 110km/h makes it not only the fastest feline but also the swiftest land animal.

This elegant creature carries its beautiful spotted frame and long, ringed tail with supermodel poise. It is much lighter in build than the leopard, with which it is sometimes confused. It also differs by having solid spots rather than rosettes, and a smaller head adorned with distinctive 'tear' marks beneath the eyes. Unlike other cats, the cheetah has unsheathed claws, which act like runner's spikes.

Wide open spaces

The cheetah is primarily a cat of open plains, although it can also survive in other habitats from open woodland to semi-desert. It remains widespread in east and southern Africa wherever the habitat is suitable, but only at very low densities. In north Africa it is very rare. Cheetahs were once also found in Asia, as far east as India: today a small population of perhaps 60 adults remains on the central Iranian plateau.

Fast food

This feline Ferrari is the most specialised big cat. It hunts by day, using sight, and relies on blinding speed to catch its prey. Keeping to cover, it stalks to within striking distance before hitting the gas – then accelerates so fast that even the speediest antelope can be run down in a matter of strides. But the tank quickly runs dry: a cheetah gives up if it hasn't succeeded within 300m.

Breeding males compete with one another for prime hunting territory and access to females. They may wander widely before settling down, sometimes ganging together in twos or threes, which helps them to see off intruders and capture larger prey. Subordinates in these gangs may get few mating opportunities but still get a better deal than if they went solo.

A female hides her cubs for at least their first month and moves them regularly. After six weeks they follow her everywhere, except on a hunt. Families feed together, the mother licking her offspring clean afterwards while purring loudly. At six months, the mother may present her cubs with live gazelle fawns or hares on which to hone their hunting skills.

Always something new
Philip Briggs

The notion of Africa being discovered by outsiders is overtly Eurocentric. A mass of palaeontological and genetic evidence now confirms Darwin's once contentious theory that our species evolved in tropical Africa. Which means, in the prehistoric long run, that it was Africans who discovered the rest of the world, not the other way around. More to the point – and rather thrillingly – it would also suggest that the ancestors of the most elusive of contemporary African creatures, from the Congo peacock to the mountain gorilla, must have lived in close proximity to our ancient ancestors for literally millions of years before the latter undertook that fateful trans-Saharan exodus.

The elephants that carried Hannibal across the Alps belonged to a North African race that has subsequently been hunted to extinction, while temple paintings near Luxor indicate that a maritime trade in ivory from East Africa dates back to the Pharaonic Era. More surprisingly, the first written report of Africa's great apes dates back to ancient Carthage – and it has been postulated that such mythical beasts as the unicorn, mermaid, phoenix and dragon derive from garbled reports of flesh-and-blood African creatures (the oryx, dugong, flamingo and monitor lizard respectively).

▲ *Sennutem ploughing with cattle: Ancient Egyptian tomb painting. New Kingdom, 1550–1069 BC.*

Fast-forward to the historic era and, where African wildlife is concerned, it remains difficult to draw a clear line between the scientifically known and the unknown. For instance, we often forget that lion, cheetah and leopard, now almost exclusively associated with sub-Saharan Africa, still roamed the Mediterranean hinterland 2,000 years ago, and were well known to the ancient Egyptians, Romans and Greeks.

Hanno the Navigator

Arguably the most ambitious naval expedition of ancient times was undertaken by the Carthaginian navigator Hanno, who sailed a fleet of 60 ships along Africa's west coast past the Gambia River to a large volcano widely since identified as Mount Cameroon. Hanno saw many hippos and crocs along the way, but his most memorable encounter was with a tribe of hairy mute 'savages' known locally as gorillas. Three females were killed and, according to Pliny the Elder, their coats were displayed in a temple in Carthage for decades afterwards. Incredibly, however, the substance behind this legend was confirmed only in 1847 when the aptly named Thomas Staughton Savage obtained a specimen in Liberia.

▲ *Hanno on elephant (unknown Italian artist, 17th century)*

'Gorilla on the attack': An early Belgian magazine cover depicts fantasies of the Congo.

And yet … a mere 200 years ago, much of the African interior remained a cartographic blank. In 1850, reports of Africa's snow-capped equatorial mountains were greeted by open mirth in Europe, while geographic convention submerged East Africa's trio of great lakes beneath a single slug-shaped inland sea. And it was only in 1847 that gorillas were elevated from the realm of ancient Carthaginian legend to hard science. Of course people – local people, that is, not Western scientists – have always lived in the shadow of Kilimanjaro, on the shores of the great lakes and alongside gorillas in the rainforest.

By the end of the 19th century the majority of Africa's large mammals had been documented by science. But not all. Among the more prominent creatures to enter the taxonomic roster in the first decade of the 20th century were the okapi, mountain gorilla, giant forest hog and mountain nyala, while more recently described primate species include Allen's swamp monkey (1923), Sanje crested mangabey (1979) and sun-tailed monkey (1984).

William Burchell

Most familiar today as the eponym of Burchell's zebra and coucal, William John Burchell (1781–1863) was responsible for the most extensive collection of African biological specimens ever assembled by one person. It consisted of 50,000 items, ranging from bulbs to skeletons, and was acquired over the course of a 7,000km expedition through unexplored parts of southern Africa starting in 1811. Supplemented by fine illustrations and copious notes, Burchell's collection was shipped back to England in 48 crates in 1815, and formed the basis of his classic two-volume work *Travels in the Interior of Southern Africa*. Much of it is now housed in Kew Botanical Garden and Oxford University Museum.

And by the end of the 20th century? Well, astonishingly, the kipunji, a highly vocal southern Tanzanian highland monkey long known to locals, eluded Western researchers until as recently as 2003. Sadly, this Mohican-sporting primate, placed in its own genus *Rungwecebus*, gained immediate international prominence by shooting straight into the Endangered category of the IUCN Red Data list. Fewer than 1,000 individuals, split between two forests, are estimated to remain.

For the romantically minded, the discovery of the kipunji lends some credibility to other legendary East African beasts: there's a horse-sized, man-eating felid of coastal forest known locally as *mngwa*; furry red troops of chimp-like *ogogwe* from the remote Wembere Steppe; and the famous brain-sucking 'Nandi bear' of western Kenya. In truth, these outsized oddities are almost certainly mythical or extinct. But at a less dramatic level – butterflies, birds, bats, bushbabies – new African species are still being discovered and described with amazing regularity, particularly in biodiversity hotspots such as the Cape Floral Kingdom, Albertine Rift and montane forests of eastern Tanzania.

Philip Briggs is a travel writer specialising in Africa. Based in South Africa, he has written over ten guides for the Bradt series, including Tanzania, Uganda, Ethiopia, Mozambique, Ghana and Malawi.

Transvaal, 1890: Big game hunters pose around their buffalo trophy.

Background: San rock engraving from Twyfelfontein National Monument in Damaraland, Namibia, depicting a variety of animals

African elephant

Loxodonta africana

Height at shoulder: 3–3.8m (males); 2.4–3.3m (females)
Tail length: 90–140cm
Weight: 4,000–6,300kg (males); 2,500–3,500kg (females)

Big is beautiful

This African icon is the biggest living land animal, and everything about it is larger than life. Take the trunk: this extended upper lip combined with a nose is both massively powerful and remarkably delicate. It can snap branches, tear up tussocks, suck up water, caress friends and wrestle with rivals. The tusks, meanwhile, are outsized incisors that have evolved into both tools and weapons. Males have larger tusks than females, reaching lengths of 3m or more.

Other outsized attributes include huge ears that act like giant fans and legs as thick as tree trunks. And although elephants can't run or jump like other animals, their ambling walk can touch 30kph – fast enough to overtake a human athlete.

Pachyderm parade

Elephants have colonised all manner of habitats, from lush rainforests and marshes to open savannahs and even desert. Historically they ranged right across sub-Saharan Africa. Today the bush or savannah elephant occurs in fragmented populations across many parts of eastern, southern and western Africa, while the forest elephant – a smaller race, considered by some authorities to be a separate species – is confined to the tropical rainforests of west and central Africa. Numbers of both have declined dramatically in the past half century, perhaps by as much as 80%. Today around half a million remain.

Africa's architect

Only our own species has had a greater impact on the environment than elephants, which mould and modify their landscape through their daily routine. Contrary to popular belief, however, they do not destroy it: in fact, they create trails, keep waterholes unblocked, spread seeds, bring down food for smaller animals and fertilise soil with their dung. The paths plodded by ancestral herds were the trails used by early human travellers, ultimately becoming the roads of today. It is only in areas where elephants are confined by humans that their activities sometimes becomes unsustainable.

Elephants' appetites match their bulk: a big bull consumes up to 300kg of grub and 160 litres of water every 24 hours. Just about every type of

WHERE TO SEE IT

You have many options. Kenya's Amboseli and Tsavo National Parks are good, while Tanzania's Tarangire and Ruaha National Parks can be spectacular. Other top spots include Zambia's South Luangwa National Park, Botswana's Chobe National Park, Zimbabwe's Hwange National Park, Namibia's Etosha National Park and South Africa's Kruger National Park. Forest elephants are best seen in Gabon, particularly in Loango National Park on the Atlantic coast and Ivindo National Park in the heart of the rainforest.

THREATS

The ivory trade fuelled the elephant's massive decline over the past two centuries. By 1900 up to 1,000 tonnes were being exported annually. In the 1970s this trade accelerated and populations plummeted. Selective targeting of individuals with big tusks has profoundly damaged elephant social structures, especially when old matriarchs are lost. There has been some recovery since the ivory ban in 1990, but poaching remains a problem. Habitat loss and the blocking of traditional migration routes by cultivation sometimes leads to human–elephant conflict, with casualties on both sides.

77
EDGE RANK

vegetation is eaten, including grass, leaves, bark, twigs, roots and fruit. The constant search for sustenance often obliges elephants to migrate considerable distances.

Elephant family groups consist mostly of related mothers and their young. These may join up to form larger 'kinship groups', led by a mature matriarch. The herd's well-being relies on her leadership and she stays in charge until she dies. Males are driven out once they become sexually mature at 10–15 years, to wander alone or join temporary bachelor groups. Once they are old enough to compete for females, these males enter periodic states of high arousal, known as 'musth', when testosterone levels sky-rocket and they can become very aggressive.

Females reach sexual maturity at around 10–11 years and give birth to a single young (rarely twins) after a 22-month gestation period. Babies take a long time to develop: weaning is usually at 6–18 months, but some may nurse for six years. Life expectancy is 50–70 years.

Addax

Addax nasomaculatus

Head/body length: 120–175cm
Shoulder height: 95–115cm
Tail length: 25–35cm
Weight: 100–135kg (males); 60–90kg (females)

WHERE TO SEE IT

The largest remaining population is in Niger, where perhaps 200 still roam the deserts around the Massif de Termit, a chain of rocky outcrops in the southeast. Captive breeding and reintroduction schemes are up and running in Morocco and Tunisia. Addax are also bred at Yotvata Hai-Bar Nature Reserve in Israel for possible release in the Negev Desert. Details at: www.sahara conservation.org/web/scf_addax_profile.php

THREATS

The addax has disappeared from eight million km² of its former range. At the turn of the 20th century this species was common, and its fresh meat and leather were sold regularly in markets in Algeria. In less than 100 years, heavily armed hunters on horseback or in vehicles have virtually wiped it out, while expanding pastoral agriculture has eaten into its few remaining haunts. With the population so low, other factors, including prolonged drought, may also prove critical.

119
EDGE RANK

Sahara survivor

At first glance, the addax brings to mind a large, long-horned goat. In fact it is an antelope, and an out-and-out desert specialist that is perfectly suited to surviving the harsh conditions of the Sahara. Adaptations include over-sized hooves for easier travelling over soft sand, and super-efficient kidneys to help it extract every last drop of water from its highly concentrated urine. The short glossy coat fades from grey-brown to creamy-white in the summer, presumably to help reflect UV rays. Other distinguishing features include an X-shaped blaze across the face, and long, corkscrew horns in both sexes.

Shrinking sands

The addax lives only in sandy and stony desert areas. Its range once extended right across the Sahara from coast to coast: as recently as 1960 tracks were seen of more than 5,000 addax crossing Mauritania's Majabat sand sea in a single day. It is a damning measure of human influence that this tenacious animal has since been exterminated from eight million square kilometres. Today perhaps fewer than 500 individuals survive in isolated pockets in Niger, Chad, and possibly along the Malian–Mauritanian border. The largest numbers are between the Termit area of Niger and the Bodélé Depression in western Chad.

Cool customers

Not surprisingly the addax's daily routine revolves around keeping cool and avoiding the sun. It tends to be more active at night, especially in summer, and during the day finds some relief by digging 'scrapes' into the cool sand beneath the surface.

Addax nibble desert grasses, plus occasional herbs and acacia bushes. All their moisture comes from their food, so they are not tied to surface water. When abundant, they were known to move around in herds of up to 20, and gatherings of up to 1,000 migrated seasonally between the Sahara and the Sahel. Today they wander only as lone individuals, or in small groups of two to four.

Males defend territories and mate with more than one female, with breeding taking place all year round. Usually a single calf is born and is fully weaned at around one month old.

Hirola
Damaliscus hunteri

Head/body length: 120–205cm
Height at shoulder: 90–135cm
Tail length: 30–45cm;
Weight: 70–115kg

These grazers are constantly on the move in search of newly sprouting shoots. Males compete for mating rights, the winners collecting a harem of females. Calves are born at the start of the rains; females spend the first two weeks alone with them, when both are especially vulnerable to predators.

Professorial persona
A hirola's long face and white 'spectacle' markings recall a rather superior professor. This odd-looking, angular antelope has a sandy-beige coat and lyre-shaped horns in both sexes.

Borderline beast
Hirola frequent short-grass plains along the Kenya–Somalian border. Perhaps 600 remain in Kenya, including an introduced herd of 100 or so in Tsavo East National Park. In Somalia they may already be extinct.

WHERE TO SEE IT

The best place within the hirola's natural range is Kenya's Arewale National Reserve. Access is from the Garissa-Lamu road, but there are no visitor facilities. An easier option is Tsavo East National Park, where Hirola were introduced in 1963. This park has good visitor facilities. Details at: www.kws.org

THREATS
A major rinderpest epidemic in the mid-1980s may have triggered a population collapse. Today the spectre of disease remains, while threats also include competition with livestock, natural predation, habitat loss, drought and poaching.

37 EDGE RANK

Mountain nyala
Tragelaphus buxtoni

Head/body length: 240–260cm (males); 190–200cm (females)
Shoulder height: 120–135cm (males); 90–100cm (females); Tail length: 20–25cm
Weight: 180–300kg (males); 150–200kg (females)

Summer shine
Males of this handsome antelope look quite different from females. They are much larger, with long spiral horns and a liver-chestnut coat with pale stripes on the flanks. During the summer this coat can be as shiny as a conker, but during cooler seasons it grows much shaggier. Females are smaller, paler and hornless.

Highland wanderer
Mountain nyala formerly ranged over much of the southeast highlands of Ethiopia, but are now restricted to the Bale Massif, where about 2,500 remain. Here they live in woodland and heathland at altitudes above 2,000m, grazing and browsing on various herbs, shrubs and grasses.

Females and young form loose herds, which males join and monitor from time to time. Mating peaks in December and young are born after a gestation of eight to nine months. Calves lie low for their first two weeks, thereafter following their mothers.

WHERE TO SEE IT

Visit the Bale Mountains National Park in Ethiopia and you'd be unlucky not to find one. Now fully protected, the nyala are reasonably tolerant and good sightings are frequent. Mornings and evenings provide the best opportunities, when animals descend into hagenia forest on the lower slopes.

THREATS
Shrinking habitat and the encroachment of humanity has been responsible for the decline of this species.

201 EDGE RANK

Mountain (eastern) gorilla

Gorilla beringei beringei

Height when upright: 150–185cm (males);
130–150cm (females); **Arm span:** up to 225cm (males)
Weight: 160–210kg (males); 70–115kg (females)

Gentle giant

King Kong has a lot to answer for. Forget the terrifying chest-beating monster; in reality, the gorilla is a gentle leaf-munching giant. It is the largest of all primates: adult males are twice the weight of an average man and twice the size of females. Their barrel-chested, pot-bellied physique might not impress a fitness fanatic, but an Olympic weightlifter would envy their immense strength.

Mountain gorillas are the high-altitude race of the eastern gorilla. They have darker, longer hair than their lowland cousins to protect them against the cold at high altitudes. Females, young and immature males are all-black, but males develop a silver-grey saddle on their backs once they reach sexual maturity, and grow especially long hair on their arms. They are known as 'silverbacks'.

Cloud cover

Mountain gorillas inhabit tropical cloudforest, characterised by its hanging mists and dense ground vegetation. They are restricted to the Virunga range of

volcanoes that straddles the borders of Rwanda, Uganda and the Democratic Republic of Congo (DRC). Most live on the slopes of three dormant volcanoes, Karisimbi, Mikeno and Visoke, generally at altitudes of 2,500–3,400m. A second population lives in Uganda's Bwindi-Impenetrable National Park, but some regard these as a different race. There are about 360 mountain gorillas in the Virungas and around 300 in Bwindi.

Salad bowl

Mountain gorillas rise early after spending the night in their ground nest of folded-over vegetation. Their forest home resembles a giant salad bowl and they spend much of the day eating, with bouts of play and rest in between. Leaves, shoots and stems of thistles, wild celery and giant stinging nettles are their favourite fare (just nine plant species account for 80% of the diet), with smaller amounts of bark, roots, flowers, fruit and occasional invertebrates thrown in. Males can eat 30kg per day, females around 20kg.

These sociable giants live in stable family groups, usually of around ten animals. Each is led by a single dominant silverback and also contains females, young and black-back males. The silverback remains in charge for four to five years, before his powers wane and a younger rival ousts him. He protects the group, directs their daily foraging and sorts out any squabbles. If two groups meet, the silverback defends his family: ritualised posturing, charging and chest-beating is normally enough to resolve any dispute.

There is no distinct breeding season. Mothers give birth only once every three to five years after a gestation period very similar to our own. During her average 40-year lifespan a female may leave only two to six youngsters. Hence, declining populations recover only very slowly.

Conserving Africa's wildlife

Africa's celebrated wildlife is under siege. Though the continent is synonymous in Western minds with unspoilt wilderness, centuries of exploitation have now changed its landscape beyond recognition. Many species teeter on the edge of extinction, while the habitats that sustain thousands more are retreating before the onslaught of overpopulation, over-exploitation and climate change. Thankfully an increasing number of conservation organisations, both local and international, are working to reverse this trend. Many offer opportunities for you to become involved.

◀ **Pushed out:** The mountain gorilla's forest habitat is encroached by terrace-style agriculture.

Forest fragments

The swathe of tropical forest across equatorial Africa is shrinking fast: more than five million hectares were lost each year in the 1990s alone. Impoverished local people often have little choice but to slash, burn and farm the land to exhaustion. Yet these forests play a critical role in the planet's water and carbon cycles, removing carbon dioxide from the atmosphere and regulating rainfall patterns. Deforestation can thus bring environmental catastrophe, from desertification of the nutrient-leached soil, to drought and floods.

The consequences for forest wildlife, such as gorillas, are dire. The conservationist Dian Fossey dedicated her life to protecting the world's remaining mountain gorillas in four national parks in Rwanda and Uganda, and her legacy is the Gorilla Organization (*www.gorillas.org*). Funds raised go to help local people manage their land sustainably, as well as to train, clothe and protect the park rangers as they in turn attempt to protect the 700 remaining gorillas from yet another hazard: poachers.

It is illegal poaching that supplies the African 'bushmeat' trade – a major factor behind the recent declines of many African primates. The combination of an increased urban and overseas market, the development of more sophisticated hunting methods and the opening up of forests through logging has turned bushmeat into a major commercial enterprise – while stocks last. The Bushmeat Crisis Task Force (*www.bushmeat.org*) is working through a variety of channels to develop solutions.

Dog days

One of Africa's most threatened and misunderstood animals is the African wild dog (see p86). Persecuted relentlessly for its occasional crimes against livestock, only about 3,000 remain. Its distribution is also highly fragmented, with many populations thought to be unsustainably small. The Zimbabwe-based organisation Painted Dog Conservation (www.painteddog.org) has a rehabilitation facility as well as initiatives to work with local people in conserving the species. Visitors can become involved.

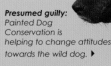

Presumed guilty: *Painted Dog Conservation is helping to change attitudes towards the wild dog.* ▶

Ill-gotten gains: Poaching elephants for ivory is still a major problem in parts of Africa ▶

Cash and conflict

In the more open landscapes of southern and eastern Africa, a similar combination of habitat loss and persecution has taken its toll on many species. Both of Africa's rhinos have suffered population crashes over the last century due to hunting – at first for sport, and more recently to supply a lucrative international market in rhino horn products. The black rhino population fell from 70,000 in the late 1960s to fewer than 2,500 in 1995, while the northern subspecies of the white rhino is virtually extinct in the wild, with just four individuals remaining in the DRC's beleaguered Garamba National Park. Save the Rhino (*www.savetherhino.org*) and the Rhino Fund Uganda (*www.rhinofund.org*) are currently working with local communities and raising funds to secure the future of both species: black rhino numbers are already starting to recover.

Meanwhile, as the human population of Africa continues to swell and habitats become more degraded, people and animals are forced to live in ever closer proximity. This inevitably leads to conflict, with animals such as elephants raiding farmland for crops. Finding ways for people and pachyderms to coexist peacefully is the challenge for scientists on one Earthwatch project in Namibia's Damaraland region. This and many other Earthwatch projects depend on the work of volunteers (*www.earthwatch.org*).

Endangered spaces

Many less publicised habitats are also imperilled, leaving entire ecosystems in jeopardy. The mangrove forests anchoring land to sea along the East African coast, for instance, constitute a vital nursery for many fish and other marine species. Yet development and urbanisation are destroying these forests, devastating wildlife communities both above the water and within it, and leaving the coastline at the mercy of erosion. The Kenya Marine and Fisheries Research Institute (*www.kmfri.co.ke*) has initiated a replanting scheme to begin to undo the damage.

The African Conservation Foundation (*www.africanconservation.org*) provides an exhaustive list of other projects under way in Africa. With determined and co-ordinated efforts and global support, many of the problems affecting Africa's spectacular fauna are now slowly but surely being brought under control.

Food for thought: Demand for bushmeat threatens many species, especially primates. ▶
Hot topic: In Zambia, fences smeared with chilli paste help deter elephants from crops. ▶
Got your number: Researchers uniquely mark wild elephants to help track their movements. ▶

Choose wisely

The choices you make as a consumer can make a real difference.

Don't:
• buy unsustainable products, such as corals, wild-collected flowers or goods made from tropical hardwoods.

Do:
• buy your African holiday via Sustainable Travel International (*www.sustainabletravelinternational.org*)
• use local expertise and meet African people when you visit, to support local economies and build understanding between cultures
• buy Fairtrade products, like Tanzanian coffee (*www.fairtrade.org.uk*) and products from sustainable sources, like cotton clothing from Wildlifeworks (*www.wildlifeworks.com*)

Madagascar

Madagascar defines 'evolutionary distinctiveness'. Its long geographical isolation has effectively turned the island into a living laboratory of evolution. The vast majority of its species have evolved in splendid isolation, following paths far removed from blueprints elsewhere. Most of them are endemic – in other words, they live nowhere else on earth.

 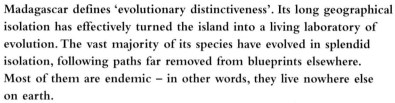

The mammals illustrate this perfectly. If you discount bats – which can fly, and so cross oceans from elsewhere – then every one of the island's native terrestrial mammals is endemic. Most famous are the lemurs, Madagascar's unique primates, of which there are 86 known species and perhaps more awaiting discovery.

Sadly, Madagascar also epitomises the spectre of 'globally endangered'. Since the arrival of humans roughly 2,000 years ago, our species has ravaged the island's forests. Today less than 15% remains, and half of what has gone has disappeared in the last 50 years.

   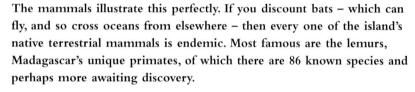

Such ecological carnage has inevitably taken its toll and many spectacular species have become extinct. These include three pygmy hippopotamuses, numerous large lemurs, and – perhaps most famously – the elephant bird (*Aepyornis maximus*), the largest bird ever to have lived.

In a nutshell, Madagascar effectively coins the EDGE concept: all of its species are evolutionarily distinct and most are now globally endangered. It is not surprising, therefore, that 11 of the EDGE top 100 species are from Madagascar, and that the island has thus claimed a chapter all to itself.

◀ *The golden-crowned sifaka is one of the world's rarest primates. Currently none of its restricted habitat is protected.*

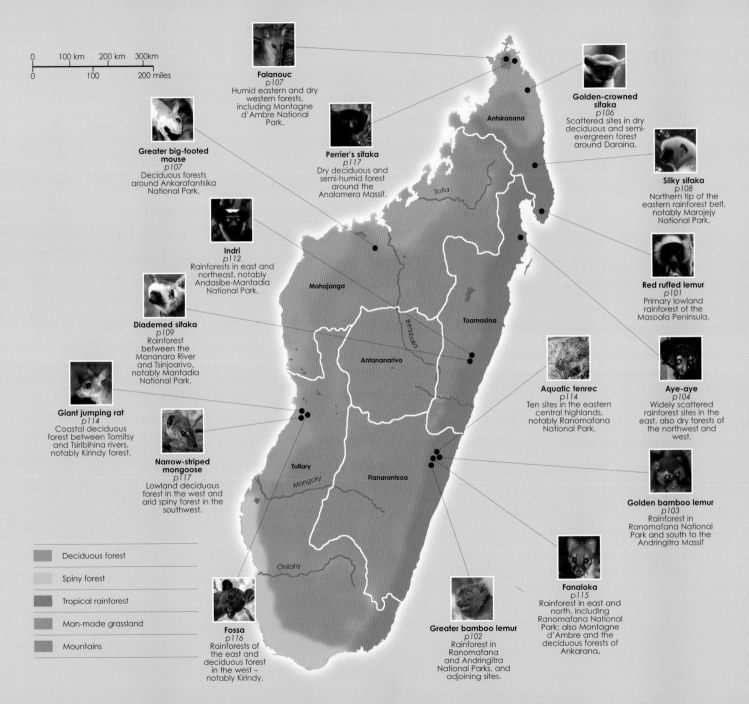

Falanouc
p107
Humid eastern and dry western forests, including Montagne d'Ambre National Park.

Golden-crowned sifaka
p106
Scattered sites in dry deciduous and semi-evergreen forest around Daraina.

Greater big-footed mouse
p107
Deciduous forests around Ankarafantsika National Park.

Perrier's sifaka
p117
Dry deciduous and semi-humid forest around the Analamera Massif.

Silky sifaka
p108
Northern tip of the eastern rainforest belt, notably Marojejy National Park.

Indri
p112
Rainforests in east and northeast, notably Andasibe-Mantadia National Park.

Red ruffed lemur
p101
Primary lowland rainforest of the Masoala Peninsula.

Diademed sifaka
p109
Rainforest between the Mananara River and Tsinjoarivo, notably Mantadia National Park.

Aquatic tenrec
p114
Ten sites in the eastern central highlands, notably Ranomafana National Park.

Aye-aye
p104
Widely scattered rainforest sites in the east, also dry forests of the northwest and west.

Giant jumping rat
p114
Coastal deciduous forest between Tomitsy and Tsiribihina rivers, notably Kirindy forest.

Narrow-striped mongoose
p117
Lowland deciduous forest in the west and arid spiny forest in the southwest.

Golden bamboo lemur
p103
Rainforest in Ranomafana National Park and south to the Andringitra Massif

Fanaloka
p115
Rainforest in east and north, including Ranomafana National Park; also Montagne d'Ambre and the deciduous forests of Ankarana.

Fossa
p116
Rainforests of the east and deciduous forest in the west – notably Kirindy.

Greater bamboo lemur
p102
Rainforest in Ranomafana and Andringitra National Parks, and adjoining sites.

Deciduous forest

Spiny forest

Tropical rainforest

Man-made grassland

Mountains

0   100 km   200 km   300km
0   100   200 miles

Antsiranana

Sofia

Mahajanga

Betsiboka

Toamasina

Antananarivo

Toliary

Mangoky

Fianarantsoa

Onilahy

Red ruffed lemur

Varecia rubra

Head/body length: 500–550mm
Tail length: 600–650mm; Weight: 3.3–3.6kg

WHERE TO SEE IT

This is not a difficult animal to see, but reaching the best spots on the Masoala Peninsula requires effort. You must obtain a permit and a guide from the park offices in Maroantsetra, and then arrange a boat to cross the Bay of Antongil to the prime sites at Andranobe, Lohatrozona and Tampolo, the last of which has rustic lodges (*www.masoalamadagascar.com*). In all locations the forest trails can be steep, wet and tough, but with the expert help of your guide you should see the lemurs. Details at: www.wcs.org/international/africa/madagascar/masoala

THREATS

Principally forest clearance and hunting. This lemur is highly susceptible to timber extraction, since the large fruiting trees on which it depends are always the first to be removed. It is also still widely hunted on the Masoala Pensinsula, despite this being a national park, especially at the onset of its calling 'period' when it becomes easier to locate. Some are also trapped for the pet trade.

115 EDGE RANK

Chestnut charmer

Warm afternoon light brings a lustrous glow to the fur of this beautiful animal as it perches in its treetop home. As well as its luxuriant coat, which varies from deep chestnut-red to honey-blonde, it also sports a very long, thick tail that serves as a wraparound scarf when the weather turns nasty.

The red ruffed lemur is familiar to many as a zoo favourite. In the wild, however, it has a very restricted range, being almost completely confined to the primary lowland rainforest of northeast Madagascar's Masoala Peninsula. Its total range is probably no more than 4,000km², with population densities varying from 21–53 animals per km².

Penthouse primate

Only the penthouse suite is good enough for this fussy feeder, which lives almost entirely in the crowns of tall trees. The reason is simple: 88% of its diet consists of fruit. With outstanding agility, sometimes even hanging upside down by its hind feet, it can pluck juicy morsels that lie beyond the reach of other lemurs. Females also eat leaves for extra protein during pregnancy and lactation.

This lemur also has a good voice, especially during summer, when animals interact with one another more regularly. It lives in mixed-sex communities that vary seasonally in size and composition. Home ranges are large (about 23–58ha), although much time is spent inside a smaller core area where the largest fruiting trees occur. Males spend most of the year here; females range more widely during the hot rainy season (January–March). Both sexes scent-mark their home ranges, sometimes by repeatedly rubbing themselves against branches.

The red ruffed lemur is one of the few diurnal lemurs to build a nursery nest of twigs and leaves. Females usually have twins or triplets, and these stay in the nest during their early stages. Later their mother carries them in her mouth to different locations. At 70 days they can move around the canopy independently.

Greater bamboo lemur

Prolemur simus

Head/body length: 400–420mm
Tail length: 450–480mm
Weight: 2.2–2.5kg

Pandering primate

A voracious appetite for bamboo makes this lemur Madagascar's answer to the giant panda. It is easily told from other bamboo lemurs by its larger size and distinct ear tufts. Its dense coat is sooty grey-brown, with russet tinges and olive-brown patches around the neck and shoulders, a creamy-brown throat and belly and a dark grey tail.

Bamboozled!

Home for this lemur must have plenty of giant bamboo. Its preferred habitat is lowland and montane rainforest up to around 1,100m, and occasionally adjacent plantations. It is now almost entirely confined to a small area in southeast Madagascar, comprising Ranomafana and Andringitra National Parks, some sites in the forest corridor connecting the two, and forest fragments to the east and south.

Subfossils tell us that this lemur was once widespread. Remains have been found in the far north, the northwest and the extreme west. It was also recorded from the northeastern rainforests during the 19th century and very recently its presence has been suspected in forests in the central east.

Cracking dinner

The greater bamboo lemur is mainly active by day but may also get around after dark. It lives in groups of up to 11, containing two or more adult males and females. Home ranges may be up to 60ha, although the lemurs tend to use only about 20% of this at a time.

True to its name, bamboo – especially giant bamboo – makes up 95% of this animal's diet. As the seasons change it selects different parts of the plant: during the rainy season (mid-November to March) sprouting shoots are favourite; from mid-April branch shoots are increasingly eaten; and between July and November it develops a taste for the inner pith. Powerful jaws allow it to crack through bamboo poles, stripping the outer layers to reach the pith and leaving behind ravaged stands of bamboo.

Mating occurs in May and June, and a single offspring is born in October or November after a gestation of around 149 days. Mothers carry their infants until around four months, after which they move independently. Weaning takes place at seven to eight months and offspring disperse from their parental group at three to four years.

WHERE TO SEE IT

This lemur is found in both Andringitra and Ranomafana National Parks, although only the latter is realistically accessible. Here you may find groups in stands of giant bamboo around the main trail network in Talatakely. The compulsory park guides, which you can arrange at the entrance gate, are very skilled at finding lemurs.

THREATS

This species' specific habitat requirements – areas with prolific stands of giant bamboo – and very small range leave this species highly vulnerable to the continuing destruction of forests for fuel and agriculture. It is regarded as one of the 25 most endangered primates in the world.

=23
EDGE RANK

Golden bamboo lemur

Hapalemur aureus

Head/body length: 340–380mm
Tail length: 380–420mm
Weight: 1.25–1.65kg

WHERE TO SEE IT

Ranomafana National Park in southeast Madagascar is the best site and was created after the discovery of the golden bamboo lemur in 1991. Look around Talatakely (the main tourist area) in stands of giant bamboo beside the main trail. An expert local guide (arranged at the park gate) will help you find them.

THREATS

Forest clearance, for timber, fuel and rice cultivation, is the most pressing threat. Bamboo is also harvested for building and other local uses. These threats are made all the more acute by the species' restricted range and its very specific habitat requirements.

=23 EDGE RANK

Good as gold

You may find this medium-sized lemur sharing the same neighbourhood as the greater bamboo lemur. But you can easily tell it from its larger cousin by the gorgeous colours of its soft, dense coat: rich olive-chestnut above and golden-brown on the chest, belly and inner limbs. The small round ears are also golden brown, while the tail is darker towards the tip. Other distinctive features include a rotund body, short muzzle and long thick tail.

Bamboozled – again!

Like its larger cousin, this species never strays far from bamboo – especially giant bamboo. It makes its home in primary mid-altitude and higher-altitude rainforest where this plant grows in abundance. Its total range covers no more than 2,500km², extending from northern areas of Ranomafana National Park south, through a narrow forest corridor, to the northeastern slopes of the Andringitra Massif. Only about 2,000 individuals are thought to remain.

Fussy feeders

This lemur is mostly active by day. Groups forage in the early morning and late afternoon, taking a rest in the middle of the day. Each group comprises an average of three to six animals, with an adult male and female, their youngsters and babies. Their territory may cover about 30ha, though they rarely travel more than 400m in a day.

Golden bamboo lemurs do not just eat any old bamboo. Giant bamboo is a particular favourite, and they are also partial to bamboo creeper and bamboo grass. They seek out the bases of young leaves and new shoots – thus reducing competition with the greater bamboo lemur, which prefers the stems and inner pith. The young shoots, though rich in protein, also contain toxic cyanide at levels powerful enough to kill a human infant. The golden bamboo lemur has evolved a special digestive system to deal with this, meaning it gets this food all to itself.

Females give birth to a single offspring in November/December after a gestation period of 138 days. At first infants shelter in dense tangles of vegetation; later their mothers 'park' them while they go to forage. Youngsters remain in their family group for three years before becoming independent.

Aye-aye

Daubentonia madagascariensis

Head/body length: 300–370mm
Tail length: 440–530mm
Weight: up to 2.5kg

Mix and match

This bizarre creature looks like some evolutionary experiment gone wrong – an animal cobbled together from the leftover parts of others. Imagine a witch's cat with rabbit's teeth, leathery bat's ears, a bushy tail and fingers like Edward Scissorhands. That's the aye-aye: a top contender for world's weirdest animal.

In reality this unmistakable primate is simply the largest of the nocturnal lemurs. It also sports long, dark, coarse fur and a cat-like face with piercing orange eyes. Its hallmark hands have elongated digits with curved claw-like nails and an extraordinarily thin middle finger that serves as a probe.

Back from the brink

Thirty years ago this animal was regarded as virtually extinct: fewer than 50 were thought to live in lowland rainforests near Mananara in northeast Madagascar. Remarkably, this proved to be completely wrong and the aye-aye may even have the broadest range of any lemur. It is versatile, too, inhabiting low- and mid-altitude rainforests, dry deciduous forests and even cultivated areas like coconut and lychee plantations.

Finger tapping

Aye-ayes are loners most of the time, but occasionally feed in pairs. By day they snooze in a treetop nest made from intertwining twigs and dead leaves. At dusk they awake, though may not become active until three hours after dark. They spend most of the night foraging restlessly in the crowns of trees, making frequent short, high-

pitched calls and travelling as much as 4km before retiring. Their odd appearance belies their impressive agility in the branches.

The aye-aye's trademark is its unique way of feeding. It finds juicy insect grubs in bark and rotting wood by tapping with its middle finger and listening for movement beneath – a strategy known as 'percussion foraging'. It then gnaws a hole and winkles out the grub with its thin middle finger. This behaviour makes the aye-aye effectively Madagascar's equivalent of woodpeckers. It uses similar techniques to break into nuts and coconuts, as well as nectar and some fungus.

Males have large home ranges (125–215ha) that overlap with those of their neighbours. Female ranges are smaller (30–50ha) and separate, though they do overlap with at least one male. There is no fixed breeding season: oestrus occurs once a year and lasts only a few days. A female 'on heat' advertises her condition with distinctive calls. Several males then gather around and fight for her charms. Copulation lasts around an hour. Afterwards the female moves on and repeats her call in search of further suitors. Both males and females may mate with several partners.

Females begin breeding at three or four years and probably leave two- to three-year intervals between births. A single baby weighing about 100g is born after a gestation of 160–170 days. It stays close to its mother to learn the tricks of her trade.

16
EDGE RANK

Golden-crowned sifaka

Propithecus tattersalli

Head/body length: 450–470mm
Tail length: 420–470mm
Weight: 3.4–3.6kg

Carrot-top

The golden-crowned sifaka was first observed by biologists in 1974, but not described as a new species until 1988. This petite, elegant creature is the smallest of its kind – though capable of impressive leaps with its long hind legs. It has bright creamy-white fur, which stands out in the treetops, and a rich yellow-orange crown, with similar tinges on the shoulders, upper arms and rump.

Jigsaw pieces

The scattered patchwork of this lemur's forest home resembles a jigsaw puzzle with most of the pieces missing. It occurs only in a 44,000ha area of dry deciduous and semi-evergreen forest in northeast Madagascar, mainly between the Manambato and Loky rivers and around the town of Daraina 55km northwest of Vohemar. Here it shows a marked preference for elevations below 500m and can be quite common in some forest patches. The total population is probably no more than 2,400–4,000 breeding adults.

A new leaf

This beautiful lemur is active during the day and spends the night sleeping in taller trees. It is a sociable animal, with groups containing three to ten animals. There may be two or more mature members of each sex but only one female breeds successfully each year, and males move between neighbouring groups during the mating season.

A group's home range varies from 6–12ha with the seasons: during drier months when meals are harder to come by, they travel further. Their diet is varied, with unripe fruits, seeds, shoots, mature leaves and flowers regularly on the menu. Bark is also eaten during the dry season. Fresh young leaves are a favourite and animals search far and wide to find them.

Golden-crowned sifakas mate in January and give birth in July, every second year. At first babies cling to their mother's belly, but they move round to ride on her back when a little older. Weaning occurs at around five months and coincides with an abundance of high-quality young leaves in the forest. By one year, young animals have reached around 70% of adult body weight.

WHERE TO SEE IT

Most forest patches or fragments around the town of Daraina contain golden-crowned sifakas. Perhaps best are those close to the village of Andranotsimaty, 5km northeast of Daraina, where some habituated groups can be approached. Contact the conservation organisation FANAMBY (*www.fanamby.org.mg*) in Daraina to arrange a guide and find out the best sites.

THREATS

Slash and burn agriculture, uncontrolled grass fires and wood extraction are rife in the Daraina area and put considerable pressure on this species' limited habitat. Further, the area is extensively mined for gold, which severely degrades the forest. However, increased levels of hunting by immigrant gold and precious gem miners now pose the greatest single threat to its long-term survival. A national park is planned for the area.

29
EDGE RANK

Greater big-footed mouse

Macrotarsomys ingens

Head/body length: 115–150mm
Tail length: 190–240mm; **Weight:** 50–75g

Tell-tail

This small, typically shaped mouse has conspicuous large ears and an extraordinarily long tail that ends in a small tuft. It is sandy brown in colour with a creamy-white belly. At present it is known only from deciduous forests in a small region of northwest Madagascar around Ankarafantsika National Park.

Burrows to treetops

Like many mice, this species is a creature of the night. By day, it sleeps alone in burrows. You can recognise these from the small piles of soil thrown up outside the entrance, which it always keeps closed. At night it emerges to climb and scurry amongst narrow branches and vines, sometimes several metres above the ground. It often pauses to rest in small forks in the branches.

WHERE TO SEE IT

Ampijoroa, in Ankarafantsika National Park, is the only site. Park guides will help you search at night along narrow branches and tangles of vines. Look for its faint reflective eye-shine in your torch beam.

THREATS

Deforestation and forest fires within its extremely restricted range pose a major threat. Direct predation from feral cats and dogs is also a problem.

38 EDGE RANK

Falanouc

Eupleres goudotii

Head/body length: 450–650mm
Tail length: 220–260mm; **Weight:** 2.5–4.5kg

Swampy

This stocky, trundling, cat-sized carnivore has the formidable front limbs of an animal built for digging. Other notable features include a small head, conical snout, large ears and fat tail. Its greyish to light brown coat is tinged russet around the thighs.

Falanoucs are sparsely distributed in the humid eastern and dry western forests of Madagascar, mostly in riverine and swampy areas.

Worm storage

Earthworms top the falanouc menu. They use their strong forepaws and long claws to dig up the leaf litter, then root around for food with their long snout. By day they sleep under logs or in rock crevices. After dark they come out to forage – usually alone. A female gives birth to one or two young between November and January. They emerge with open eyes and a full coat of fur, and can follow their foraging mother within two days.

During the bountiful wet summer the Falanouc stores large amounts of fat in its thick tail. This helps it survive the winter, when earthworms are much harder to find.

WHERE TO SEE IT

Tricky. This animal is shy, nocturnal and rare. In Montagne d'Ambre National Park at Madagascar's northern tip, you might occasionally spot one at night close to the Station Roussettes. Guides at the park entrance will help.

THREATS

Forest destruction, forest fires and the draining of wetland areas are the most serious. Predation by dogs and hunting for meat are also a concern.

90 EDGE RANK

Silky sifaka

Propithecus candidus

Head/body length: 480–540mm
Tail length: 450–510mm
Weight: 5–6.5kg

Snowball

It seems incongruous to peer into the gloomy depths of a rainforest and see a bright white lemur sat in a tree. Quite why the silky sifaka should be that colour is a mystery, though its thick coat undoubtedly protects it from regular deluges. The creamy-white fur sometimes has tints of silver-grey around the crown, back and limbs. Peculiarly, some individuals lack pigment on their faces and other areas, leaving patches of pink or slate-grey skin. Males also have a large brown 'chest patch', which has been worn bare by scent marking using a gland in that region.

Lemur with altitude

The silky sifaka lives in mid-altitude and montane rainforest, preferring elevations above 700m and occasionally up to 1,600m. It is found only at the very north of the eastern rainforest belt, from Marojejy, around Andapa Basin to Anjanaharibe-Sud, and then south possibly to the region of Ambodivoahangy. This covers a total area of no more than 2,250km².

Rain stops play

The silky sifaka is active during the day and lives in groups of two to nine individuals. Smaller groups comprise an adult pair plus their offspring, while larger groups contain more than one breeding pair plus their juveniles. Females lead the group and direct its movements.

Feeding can begin at dawn but in poor weather the sifakas often continue to snooze. Just less than half the day is spent resting in the treetops, one quarter feeding, and the remainder travelling and playing. During rest periods they also groom and play with favourite partners.

Silky sifakas are specialist leaf eaters: over 75% of the diet is mature or young leaves, 15% fruit and seeds and 7% flowers, with occasional bark and soil making up the remainder.

Mating occurs between November and January and the young are born in June or July. Infants initially cling to their mother's belly, but after a month move to ride on her back, jockey-style. All group members interact with infants, including grooming, playing, carrying and nursing.

WHERE TO SEE IT

The only accessible location for this extremely rare creature is Marojejy National Park, where the best areas are between Camp Marojejia (Camp 2) and Camp Simpona (Camp 3). Marojejia is a five- to six-hour walk from the Sambava–Andapa road, Simpona a further three hours. There are well-maintained rustic huts with bunk beds, toilets and showers at each camp (*www.marojejy.com*).

THREATS

People hunt this lemur for food, particularly around northern and western parts of Marojejy (and even within the park), and other areas around the Andapa Basin. Mining in the area has exacerbated this problem. Forest destruction, even within park boundaries, also continues, especially the extraction of valuable hardwoods such as ebony and rosewood.

No ranking
EDGE RANK

Diademed sifaka

Propithecus diadema

Head/body length: 500–550mm
Tail length: 440–500mm
Weight: 6–8.5kg

WHERE TO SEE IT

The most accessible locality for this gorgeous animal is Mantadia National Park, 15km north of Andasibe in eastern Madagascar. Some groups are habituated and good sightings are increasingly common, though not guaranteed. National park guides are obligatory, and can be arranged at the park entrance. They often work in tandem with other guides to increase your chances of success.

THREATS

Habitat loss and hunting for food are the two most severe threats. Forest at the southern extreme of its range is cleared to make way for sugar cane used in illegal rum production.

156
EDGE RANK

Beauty queen

This elegant animal would scoop first prize in any beauty pageant for lemurs. Its winning combination of long limbs, inquisitive eyes and gorgeous colours would surely overwhelm the judges.

The silky coat alone is exceptional: typically slate-grey on the shoulders and upper back, fading to silver-grey lower down and white on the tail. Its arms and legs are rich orange to gold, with black hands and feet, while the white head is offset by a black skullcap, a bare grey face and penetrating rich, red-brown eyes.

Some individuals in the far southwest of its range are darker, generally with a black head, shoulders, hands and feet, slate-grey on the upper body and upper arms, and fiery orange limbs.

Eastern promise

This lemur inhabits mid-altitude rainforest up to around 1,700m, favouring elevations above 700m. It is found only in the rainforests of the east and northeast, though the precise limits are uncertain. The northern limit is probably the region of the Mananara River, west to the Marotandrano Massif, while the southern limit is the vicinity of Tsinjoarivo, and corresponds to the west–east line formed by the Onive River and lower reaches of the Mangoro.

Salad bar

A typical day for the diademed sifaka involves time spent at all levels of the forest canopy – and even occasionally on the ground, where it searches for fallen fruits, fungi and soil, and indulges in play-wrestling bouts with companions. Its diet is a super salad, comprising immature leaves, fruit seeds, whole fruits and flowers. Over 25 different plant species are eaten daily, the proportions varying with seasonal abundance. Foraging may take it 500–1,700m in a day.

Social groups of up to eight or more include several adult males and females that have home ranges of 25–60ha (groups in forest fragments have smaller ranges). Group composition changes over time as both sexes migrate between groups. Sifakas call in order to keep the group together, as well as to convey aggression and signal alarm. Both infants and adults sometimes fall prey to fossas.

Mating takes place between January and March, with births occurring in June. At first the single offspring clings to its mother's lower belly, progressing to riding on her back when older.

Fear and loathing in Madagascar

Hilary Bradt

Vari ou Singe

Pingun

Imagine being the first man to set foot in Madagascar. We don't know for sure where he came from, but we do know that it was only a couple of thousand years ago. Imagine his sturdy outrigger canoe driven by the trade winds to the west coast of this huge island which, as far as he knew, could be the shores of a new continent. Imagine him stepping warily ashore and looking around, examining the bizarre spiny tendrils of the octopus trees and gazing up at the towering baobabs. He is hungry, thirsty and terrified. If the plants are monsters, what other fearsome creatures might be hidden in their depths?

It is in the nature of humankind to fear the unknown, but in fact Madagascar at that time was as close to paradise as you can get. The first people found no dangerous animals but plenty of edible ones. In the swampy areas they speared rotund, shiny black animals laden with meat. It is the butchered bones of these pygmy hippos, now extinct, that tell us when the first humans arrived.

A few centuries later came the first waves of immigrants from Indonesia. They brought women, rice and later cattle, and retreated to the safety of the highlands, confining the monsters to the lowland forests. And monsters they were, but not fearsome ones. Archaeologists have found the bones of

16 prehistoric lemurs, all larger than any present-day species, and the towering elephant bird which gave rise to Marco Polo's stories of the roc. So when the first Europeans arrived in the 17th century they had already heard stories of strange animals. And since travellers' tales are no good without a few monsters, these chroniclers got to work with gusto.

'The baboon grows to an enormous size'

One of the earliest chroniclers of Madagascar was Sieur (Sir) de Bois, who was sent to the island in 1669 by King Louis X1V. Perhaps his persistent suffering from malaria explains the hallucinatory nature of his wildlife observations: 'There are some birds the size of a large turkeycock', he wrote, 'which have the head made like a cat and the rest of the body like a griffin; these birds hide themselves in the thick woods, and when anyone passes under the tree where they are they let themselves fall so heavily on the head of the passengers that they stun them, and in the moment they pierce their heads with their talons, then they eat them.'

Nearly two centuries later, Samuel Copland gave his imagination similar rein in his *A History of the Island of Madagascar*. One observation, however, may be more plausible: 'The baboon grows to an enormous size … at least seven feet high when standing on its hind legs. It is a very savage and intractable animal and its imperfect and hideous resemblance to the human form gives it a horrific appearance.' Copland never visited Madagascar but could this description have evolved from an eyewitness account of one of the now-extinct giant lemurs? *Megaladapis*, for one, is described as having been the size of a gorilla.

Hypopotami

Heron   *Fanu*

There were plenty of accurate accounts among the wilder stories. The earliest description of some of the island's wildlife was penned in 1609 by a German who accurately describes ring-tailed lemurs. Etienne Flacourt, a French governor writing in 1658, was also spot on when it came to lemurs, although his descriptions of rhinoceros and penguins are hard to swallow. A British contemporary, Walter Hamond, who was more interested in promoting colonisation than terror, noted – accurately – that 'Beasts of prey, as lions, tigers, woolves, and the like we saw none.'

The fascination with the wildlife of Madagascar continued into the 18th century. In 1771 a young French doctor,

Joseph-Philibert Commerson, spent three months in the south of the island, and wrote to his tutor in Paris: 'I have truly found the naturalist's promised land. Nature seems to have retreated into a private sanctuary to work on models unlike any she has created elsewhere. At every step one encounters the most strange and marvellous forms.'

It was the arrival of the missionary naturalists, most notably James Sibree from Queen Victoria's Britain, that brought measured, scientific study of the wildlife of Madagascar, a process that continues to this day. And the facts about the animals that live in 'nature's private sanctuary' have turned out to be as strange as any fiction.

Falanwuc

THE AYE-AYE.

[The Aye-Aye (*Cheiromys Madagascariensis*).]

From church to forest: James Sibree

The young architect James Sibree was originally sent to Madagascar in 1863 to oversee the building of the Martyr Memorial Churches in the capital. He returned as an ordained minister in 1870 and ended up spending 50 years on the island. His five books include *A Naturalist in Madagascar*, and there is no better 19th century writer on the island's people and wildlife. Typical of his insight is this observation about an aye-aye kept at the zoo in Regents' Park that, in declining an array of insects, convinced its keeper that the species was not carnivorous. 'Possibly,' responds Sibree, 'the explanation is to be found in the fact that none of the insects of England which were offered to the aye-aye were suitable to its taste. It therefore preferred another kind of food to starvation.'

◀ An early engraving of the aye-aye printed in 'The Penny Magazine of the Society for the Diffusion of Useful Knowledge' in 1838.

Hilary Bradt is the author of three books on Madagascar, and co-author of Madagascar Wildlife. She has visited the island more than 30 times as a tour leader and as a lecturer on board expedition cruise ships. Other lecture venues include the Smithsonian Institution in Washington and the Royal Geographical Society in London.

Indri
Indri indri
Size: 640–720mm; Weight: 6–9kg

WHERE TO SEE IT

Seeing this spectacular creature should be compulsory for any visitor to Madagascar. In Analamazaotra Reserve (part of Andasibe-Mantadia National Park) two family groups are completely habituated and good sightings are virtually guaranteed; be in the forest from 07.00–10.00 to hear them call. You can also try nearby Mantadia National Park, though larger territories here make the indris harder to locate. The park guides at Andasibe are very good and will help you arrange trips to both sites.

THREATS

The ongoing felling of the rainforest, to supply local fuel and timber and clear land for cultivation, remains the greatest threat to this species – even within some protected areas. Historically, indris were protected from hunting by local beliefs (known as *fady*). In many areas these beliefs have now broken down, partly due to the immigration of other ethnic groups, leaving indris increasingly vulnerable to hunting for their meat and skins.

36
EDGE RANK

Ancestral songster

Imagine a large black-and-white teddy bear in a tree and you have a pretty good idea of an indri. This is both the largest of Madagascar's lemurs and the loudest, with an unforgettable wailing song that echoes eerily through its rainforest home.

Other key indri features include virtually no tail, and amazingly long hind legs to power its huge leaps through the tree canopy. It also has tufted ears, piercing yellow-green eyes, and a striking black-and-white pattern. This charismatic combination certainly made an impact on the Betsimisaraka tribe, who named the indri 'Babakoto' – literally 'ancestor of man'.

The indri is confined to rainforests in central-eastern and northeastern Madagascar, preferring elevations below 1,000m. Its range extends from Anosibe An'ala region in the south to near Andapa in the north. Subfossils found in the far north and the central highlands suggest it was once much more widespread.

Canopy chorus

Indris form small family groups of two to six, each comprising an adult pair with their offspring. They are most active by daytime, only moving at night during bad weather or when a predator disturbs them. Each group occupies a territory of 17–40ha, which tends to be larger in big, undisturbed tracts of forest. Pairs stick together, but if one mate dies its survivor finds a new partner. Females are dominant over males and take first pick of any food.

The Indri's signature song carries for 1–2km and neighbouring groups take turns to respond. This question-and-answer chorus keeps families well spaced out and helps prevent them from intruding on each other's space. Most singing takes place in the morning, from 07.00–11.00. During October and November, groups may also call at night.

Calling helps bring the group closer together. A singing bout typically begins with a communal 'roar' before the song proper gets under way. All group members, except very young offspring, join in. Pairs often perform synchronised duets. Bouts usually last around 45 seconds, though a really good session may take up to three minutes.

Indris are active for 5–11 hours a day, depending on the weather and season. During this time they travel an average of 700–800m in search of food,

although they take plenty of time out to rest between feeding sites. It takes them 8–14 days to cover most of their territory.

A 10m leap is nothing to an indri, which springs from branch to tree trunk in spectacular bounds as it searches for food. Up in the canopy it finds the young leaves and leaf buds that make up its staple diet, as well as a smattering of fruits, seeds and flowers. It may also descend to the ground for a quick snack of soil, which is thought to help neutralise toxins that build up from all those leaves.

Indris reach sexually maturity at seven to nine years. Females give birth only every third year, so the population grows very slowly. Mating occurs between December and March, and the single offspring is usually born in May/June after a gestation of around 150 days. At first the mother carries her infant low down on her stomach, but at four months it hops round onto her back. Youngsters can move independently at eight months, but stick close to their mother until well past their second year.

Giant jumping rat

Hypogeomys antimena

Head/body length: 305–345mm
Tail length: 215–240mm; Weight: 1.1–1.3kg

Rabbit rodent

This big brown rat has a round body, big ears and long muscular tail. It often sits upright like a rabbit and, when agitated, even hops on its hind legs like a mini kangaroo.

Once widespread, the giant jumping rat is now restricted to an 800km² strip of coastal deciduous forest between the Tomitsy and Tsiribihina rivers. There may be up to 50 individuals per km² in suitable habitat, but numbers are generally much lower than this.

Family burrower

Giant jumping rats forage for fallen fruit, seeds and leaves, strip bark from saplings, and dig for roots and tubers. Families live in burrow complexes, which provide shelter from predators, and have numerous tunnels and entrance holes. They plug the entrances with soil then excavate them in order to get in and out.

Unlike most rodents, the giant jumping rat is monogamous, pairs sticking together until one mate dies. A female gives birth to one or two young at the start of the rainy season.

WHERE TO SEE IT
Kirindy Forest, 60km northeast of Morondava, is the place. Moonless nights are best. Be prepared to search over two or three nights. See: www.birdlife.org/action/ground/arabuko/index.html

THREATS
Ongoing habitat destruction is the main threat to this species. Hunting by villagers with dogs is also a problem.

95
EDGE RANK

Aquatic tenrec

Limnogale mergulus

Head/body length: 120–170mm
Tail length: 130–160mm; Weight: 60–105g (average 80g)

Web-footed wonder

Looking like a cross between a water vole and a shrunken otter, this is Madagascar's only aquatic mammal. Adaptations for its watery lifestyle include dense fur to repel water and keep it warm, long whiskers to 'feel' food under water, and webbed toes and a keeled tail to work as propeller and rudder.

This shy insectivore inhabits fast-flowing streams at 600–2,000m. It appears to be limited to just ten sites in the eastern central highlands, ranging from just south of Lac Alaotra in the north to the upper Lantara River region in the south.

Night diver

Tenrecs are feisty little animals that battle along streambeds at night to catch insect larvae, frogs and other prey. They make short dives to the bottom, then return to the surface and consume their catch at the water's edge.

Daytime is spent in burrows beside the stream, before emerging to feed shortly after sunset. They may remain active all night, though are always back in their burrow before sunrise. Their toilet habits are meticulous, and they maintain neat latrines on prominent boulders in streams.

WHERE TO SEE IT
This rare, secretive animal is very difficult to see. Ranomafana National Park offers a chance, although it will take effort and luck. Watch out for its calling-card latrines along streams in eastern montane rainforest areas.

THREATS
Deforestation causing soil erosion and the silting of streams is a major threat. Upland forests have become highly fragmented and suitable riverside habitat is now isolated.

117
EDGE RANK

Fanaloka

Fossa fossana

Head/body length: 400–450mm
Tail length: 215–265mm
Weight: up to 1.9kg (males); 1.75kg (females)

WHERE TO SEE IT

Fanalokas are easy to see at Ranomafana National Park, where bait is put out and they have grown very tolerant of people. Park guides will take you to the right area, but be prepared for lots of other tourists. You may also occasionally see one in Ankarana Special Reserve around Campement Anilotra (Camp des Anglais), but here they are very shy. Chance encounters during night walks elsewhere are rare.

THREATS

Deforestation through conversion to cultivated land, logging and charcoal production is the most serious threat. In areas of the northeast the fanaloka is also prized as food. Introduced carnivores like dogs, cats and the small Indian civet compete for food, transmit disease and may even prey directly on the fanaloka.

257
EDGE RANK

Foxy features

This cat-sized carnivore has fox-like features, short legs and small, delicate paws. Its pale brown and grey coat is boldly spotted, with the spots becoming lines along the back and flanks. The thick, cylindrical tail is ringed with faint dark bands and diffuse spots.

Humid haven

Like most of Madagascar's endemic fauna, the fanaloka is found only in native forests. It occurs throughout rainforest areas in the east and north, from sea level to 1,600m, including the Sambirano

region in the northwest and littoral forests near Tolagnaro in the south. Some also live in the isolated humid forests of Montagne d'Ambre and drier deciduous forests of Ankarana in the north.

Riverside residence

Like most small carnivores, this species is nocturnal and shy. It spends daytime asleep in a tree hole, rock crevice or similar retreat then emerges after dark to feed on the forest floor and in low vegetation. Favourite morsels include small mammals, reptiles, frogs and invertebrates – including freshwater crabs.

Males and females live together, usually around rivers, streams and marshes. They share a territory of up to 0.5km², which they mark with their scent glands. Courtship takes place in August and September, with a single young born after a gestation period of around 85 days. Unusually for carnivores, the young are very well developed at birth: they weigh 60–70g, have their eyes open and are fully furred. Though up and walking after just three days, they are not fully weaned until two to three months.

Food can be scarce and foraging difficult during winter (June–August), so the fanaloka lays down fat reserves during summer, especially in its thick tail. This may constitute up to one quarter of its total body weight.

Fossa

Cryptoprocta ferox

Head/body length: 75–80cm (males); 65–70cm (females); Tail length: 70–90cm
Weight: 6–10kg (males); 5–7kg (females)

Lemur's nightmare

This slinky cross between a cat and a weasel is Madagascar's hunter *par excellence*. All teeth and attitude at the front end, it is a lemur's worst nightmare. Some (unfounded) myths even consider it a threat to humans.

A fossa's lithe, muscular body is supremely adapted to treetop life: its short legs, large pads, partially retractile claws and exceptionally long tail are all built for climbing. Other distinctive features include a small head with large eyes, and a smooth sepia-brown coat. Scientists once thought that the fossa was related to cats; it certainly occupies a cat-like predatory role on Madagascar. They now know, however, that it has a different ancestry and that its catlike traits arose through convergent evolution.

Fossas occur in all native forest regions from sea level to 2,600m, but their strongholds are the larger rainforest blocks of the northeast and remaining tracts of deciduous forest in the west. Their territories are large, and population densities everywhere are very low.

Born to climb

Fossas may sleep in caves or old termite mounds, but most choose trees – often slumped over a large branch. Hunting is usually at night, and fossas are equally at home in the trees or on the ground. Few other animals can match their agility: 'reversible' ankles enable them to grasp both sides of tree trunks with their hind feet when descending headfirst or leaping to an adjacent trunk.

Mammals dominate the fossa menu. In mountains they often take smaller prey like shrew tenrecs; in forests they prefer larger prey such as lemurs, which they ambush at night while sleeping. Prey is pinned down with the front paws then dispatched with a bite to the throat or back of the neck. Victims may be eviscerated and their vital organs eaten first.

Fossas are generally loners – except during the breeding season, when females flaunt themselves to passing males from the branches of a favourite tree and mate with several over a week or so. Copulation is a noisy business and, if uninterrupted by other males, can last several hours – perhaps because males have proportionately the largest penis of any mammal.

An average litter of two to four babies is born after six to seven weeks. Females are solely responsible for the upbringing of their young, which reach independence after one year and maturity two or three years later.

WHERE TO SEE IT

Fossas are seen most often in western deciduous forest, particularly Kirindy near Morondava. In eastern rainforests glimpses are extremely rare. Ankarana in northern Madagascar can also be productive. In all national parks you should have a guide, but even then sightings are a matter of luck. Do not disturb fossas if you chance upon them mating.

THREATS

The fossa's principal threat is the continued destruction of native forest. However, villagers in some areas also persecute it for taking domestic fowl, while others use body parts in traditional medicine. Packs of feral dogs sometimes kill fossas.

=43
EDGE RANK

Perrier's sifaka

Propithecus perrieri

Head/body length: 430–470mm
Tail length: 420–460mm; Weight: 3.7–5kg

Black magic

This animal has the long limbs and tail typical of the sifaka family. But its striking combination of completely jet-black coat and piercing orange-red eyes is unique.

It also has the most restricted range of any sifaka: a mere 400km² pocket of dry deciduous and semi-humid forests centred upon the Analamera Massif in far northeast Madagascar. Probably fewer than 1,000 individuals remain.

Mango muncher

Perrier's sifaka lives in small groups of about two to six, each occupying a home range of around 30ha. It eats mainly leaves, unripe fruit, young shoots and flowers. At the end of the dry season (November) groups sometimes move into riverine forest to feed in mango trees. A feeding group may spread out more than 50m, but members keep in touch with regular quiet calls.

WHERE TO SEE IT

Finding this species is a serious challenge. The forests along the Bobakindro River in Analamera offer the best chance – particularly in October–November when mango trees are fruiting. Hire a guide from the Ankarana/Analamera park office and be prepared to rough it. Tour operators in Antsiranana can help organise your trip.

THREATS

Loss of habitat through uncontrolled fires, charcoal production and forest clearance is the greatest threat for this species. The fragmentation of forest patches obliges them to cross open areas where they are vulnerable to lurking fossas and feral dogs.

No ranking
EDGE RANK

Narrow-striped mongoose

Mungotictis decemlineata

Head/body length: 250–320mm
Tail length: 200–240mm; Weight: 400–550g

Star in stripes

This dainty little mongoose has a grizzled beige coat and eight to ten dark stripes along its flanks. Its muzzle is pointed, its ears small and rounded, its legs short and its tail bushy.

Home is the lowlands, where it favours dense primary deciduous forest in the west and arid spiny forest in the southwest. Its known range lies between the Tsiribihina and Fiherenana rivers, and inland towards Mahabo.

Lovely grubs

This sociable carnivore forages in groups by day – mostly on the ground, though sometimes also in trees. It eats largely insects, and is especially partial to grubs, which it digs out from decaying wood during the dry season. In the rainy season it may also snap up small mammals, reptiles and worms.

Family units number up to 12 during the wet season (December–May), but shrink to 3–5 during the dry season (June–October). Mating takes place in August and September. The female bears a single young after a gestation period of 74–106 days and moves it in her mouth between dens.

WHERE TO SEE IT

Kirindy, northeast of Morondava, is the best place. Here it is locally quite common, and over two or three days you have a good chance of success.

THREATS

In some areas direct hunting by feral dogs is a specific problem. However, deforestation remains the biggest worry for this species. Feral dogs and cats may possibly transmit diseases.

171
EDGE RANK

Conserving wildlife in Madagascar

Madagascar is the fourth-largest and the oldest island in the world. Isolated from continental landmasses for 160 million years, its extraordinarily rich ecological heritage boasts 5% of the world's plant and animal species, the majority of which (including all its native non-flying mammals) are found nowhere else on Earth. However, nearly three-quarters of Madagascar's people live below the national poverty line, which places the land and its resources under great pressure. Over the 2,000 or so years since the first settlers arrived, the island's landscape and ecology have undergone dramatic and far-reaching changes.

A tale of two forests

Madagascar can be divided roughly in two according to its predominant forest type, with tropical rainforest in the eastern and central regions, and tropical dry forest in the west and south. The rainforest in particular has suffered massive deforestation, mainly due to small-scale but widespread slash-and-burn clearance for subsistence farming. Slash-and-burn cultivation (known locally as *tavy*) presents a complex conservation challenge, as such a high proportion of Malagasy people are impoverished and many are subsistence farmers. While, on paper, many sites are protected from such damage, in practice this protection is often meaningless. Many species, including most lemurs, are being forced into fewer and smaller fragments of forest as the habitat in which they evolved is steadily whittled away.

The cleared land is also vulnerable to surface erosion and run-off, which further threatens both its productivity and capacity for recovery. This erosion has seriously and perhaps permanently compromised the fertility of much of the central highland plateau. It is estimated that 80% of Madagascar is now heavily eroded.

The Durban Vision

The name is confusing. It has nothing to do with South Africa, but is all about a commitment made by the president of Madagascar, Marc Ravalomanana, to triple the protected areas of wildlife habitat in the space of five years. He made the announcement at the 2003 World Parks Congress in Durban. This ambitious and far-sighted policy has secured for the country another six million hectares of national parks and reserves.

▲ **Slash-and-burn:** *Small-scale forest clearance adds up to a big problem for Madagascar.*

Desert in the forest: *Many parts of Madagascar's once forested highlands are now treeless, heavily eroded wastelands.* ▶

Tourism and the poverty trap

With such a large array of unique and appealing wildlife, Madagascar has tremendous potential in the growing ecotourism market. A successful ecotourism strategy is seen by the government as a vital tool for solving the twin problems of desperate poverty and vanishing wildlife. Promoting ecotourism is one of the goals of the System of Protected Areas of Madagascar, a new park management system introduced in 2006. One of SAPM's key aims is to ensure that Malagasy communities benefit directly from ecotourism. For example, 50% of park entrance fees collected by SAPM go straight to local communities, and visitors cannot enter a park without hiring a local guide.

International conservation organisations work alongside Malagasy NGOs to ensure that local communities benefit. An example is the

◀ *Carbon footprints: Burning trees and selling the charcoal is a quick but unsustainable way to make money.*

successful project to protect the Alaotra gentle lemur which has been managed for nearly 20 years by the Durrell Wildlife Conservation Trust (*www.durrell.org*). One of their partners is Madagascar Wildlife Conservation (*www.mwc-info.net/en*) which has established Camp Bandro (*bandro* is the local name for this lemur) on the shores of Lake Alaotra, and is training villagers to act as wildlife guides. Another equally effective Malagasy NGO is FANAMBY (*www.fanamby.org.mg*) which has special responsibilities for sustainable tourism in the new protected areas.

Volunteering in Madagascar

Ranomafana National Park, located in the rainforest of southeast Madagascar, is one of the largest of Madagascar's many protected areas. Tourists interested in gaining a real insight into conservation work in Madagascar can take part in research expeditions in Ranomafana with the Earthwatch Institute (*www.earthwatch.org*), studying the park's resident Milne-Edwards sifakas. Meanwhile, responsibletravel.com offers volunteers the chance to study fossas in Ankarafantsika and Kirindy Mitea National Parks in the dry deciduous forest of western Madagascar. Blue Ventures (*www.blueventures.org*), another volunteer organisation, works with local communities to encourage sustainable management of marine ecosystems.

Madagascar's ecological heritage is unlike that of any other part of the world. Saving its unique wildlife is a matter of urgent prioroty. The political will is there, and if ways can be found to tackle the country's poverty at the same time, the potential exists for conservation success on an inspirational scale.

Burning desert

In the south of Madagascar lies a region known as the spiny desert. This has a rich biodiversity, despite the forbidding name, with extremely high levels of endemism: 95% of its plants are found nowhere else on Earth, while numerous mammals, birds and reptiles, such as Grandidier's mongoose, long-tailed ground roller and Dumeril's boa are also restricted to the specialised habitats of this region. The main threats facing this desert are the destruction of its slow-growing trees and woody plants for firewood and charcoal, and deliberate burning to clear land for grazing. The WWF (www.wwf.org), active in Madagascar since 1985, has identified several key sites within the desert in urgent need of immediate and strict protection.

▲ *Desert gems: Dumeril's boa is one of many unique and threatened species found in Madagascar's spiny desert.*

New World

The New World region constitutes sub-Arctic North America (for convenience, this book includes the Arctic within the Eurasian region), Central America and South America. Among its more spectacular features are the Amazon, which is both the world's greatest rainforest and its longest river; the Atacama Desert, which is the driest on the planet; the Andes, which is the world's longest and second-highest mountain chain; and the Great Lakes, which are the largest group of freshwater lakes on Earth.

Biodiversity within the Amazon Basin alone is staggering. Tropical rainforests occupy less than 3% of the world's surface area, but are home to more than 50% of all known animal and plant species. The Amazon is at the heart of this luxuriance and is effectively the greatest library of genetic diversity on the planet. Its colossal biomass of trees is responsible for producing a huge proportion of the atmosphere's oxygen, so damage and disruption to this ecosystem has profound global consequences.

While the New World is perhaps the least densely populated of the world's biogeographical regions, the influence of humans has been and continues to be considerable. Ever since our initial colonisation around 12,000 years ago, waves of extinctions have littered the wake of human progress. Today, the New World hosts the most profligate nation on earth, accounting for only 5% of its overall population yet consuming 30% of its energy resources.

◀ *Epitomising the North American West, a herd of bison graze in the shadow of the Grand Teton Mountains, Wyoming.*

American bison
p136
Northern and western
USA and Canada

Baird's tapir
p128
Central America:
Guatemala to
Colombia

Volcano Rabbit
p130
Sierra Nevada and
Sierra Chichinautzin,
Central Mexico

Amazonian manatee
p138
Waterways of Amazon
Basin, including Brazil,
Guyana, Columbia,
Peru and Ecuador

Spectacled bear
p131
The Andes: Venezuela
to northern Argentina

Cuban Solenodon
p123
Oriente Province,
eastern Cuba

Giant armadillo
p134
East of the Andes:
northern
Venezuela to
northern Argentina

Mountain tapir
p129
High Andes: Colombia,
Ecuador and
northern Peru

Giant river otter
p139
Northern and central
South America,
including Orinoco,
Amazon and La Plata
River systems

**Aceramarca gracile
mouse-opossum**
p124
Eastern Andes: La Paz
Department, Bolivia;
one location in Peru

**Brazilian three-banded
armadillo**
p135
Highlands of
northeastern and
central Brazil

**Short-tailed
chinchilla**
p124
Andes: confined to
northern Chile

**Maned
three-toed sloth**
p125
Bahia and Espirito
Santo states,
eastern Brazil

Andean cat
p134
High Andes: Argentina,
Bolivia, Chile and Peru

Monito del monte
p129
South-central Chile;
Neuquen and Rio
Negro provinces,
Argentina

Chacoan peccary
p130
Gran Chaco region:
western Paraguay,
southeastern Bolivia
and northern
Argentina

Maned wolf
p126
Central South
America: Brazil,
Paraguay, Peru,
Bolivia and
Argentina

Semidesert

Desert

Steppe (grass, brush and thicket)

Savanna

Deciduous forest

Tropical rainforest

Mountains

Taiga (coniferous forest)

Greenland

Canada

Rocky Mts

United States of America

USA
(Alaska)

Colorado

Missouri

Mississippi

Mexico

*Sierra
Madre*

Bahamas

Cuba
Haiti
Jamaica
Dominican
Republic
Puerto Rico

Belize
Hon.
Guatemala
El.Salvador
Nicaragua
Panama

Venezuela
Colombia
Guyana
Surinam
Fr.Guiana

Ecuador

Amazon

Brazil

Peru

Bolivia

Andes

Paraguay

Chile

Uruguay

Argentina

Cuban solenodon

Solenodon cubanus

Head/body length: approx. 280–390mm
Tail length: approx. 175–255 mm
Weight: 0.7–1kg

Ancient insectivore

The odd-looking animal resembles a super-sized shrew. It represents a primitive branch of the mammal evolutionary tree and is related to other ancient insectivores, including the tenrecs of Madagascar (see page 114).

Key features include small eyes, large naked-looking ears, a thick scaly tail and an extremely elongated snout that is supported by a rod of cartilage. Its body is covered in patchy, blackish-brown fur flecked with buff. The front legs are longer than the hind legs and equipped with powerful claws for digging.

Rising from the dead

Since its discovery in 1861 only 36 solenodons have been caught, and at various times during the past century it was thought to be extinct. More individuals were since captured in the mid-1970s and again in 2003.

This species is endemic to Cuba, and was probably once widely distributed at both the eastern and western ends of the island, though largely absent from the centre. Today it is confined to Oriente Province in eastern Cuba, where it inhabits dense humid forest and brush country up to an altitude of 2,000m.

Toxic teeth

Solenodons have very poor vision, but make up for it with a good sense of smell and excellent hearing. They are nocturnal and social, living in family groups of up to eight that spend the day in burrows, hollow trees or similar hiding places.

Their long snouts are built to root around for invertebrates, which they dig up with their strong claws. Insects, insect larvae and other invertebrates form the bulk of their diet, with some small reptiles, roots, fruit and leaves also thrown in. Uniquely among mammals, solenodons also have venomous saliva, which they inject into their prey through grooves on their incisors. This is a relatively long-lived species, but it reproduces very slowly: females typically give birth to just two single offspring in their lifetime.

WHERE TO SEE IT

Cuban solenodons are found only on Cuba, where they are known to occur within two protected reserves: Sierra del Cristal National Park in Holguin Province and Alejandro de Humboldt National Park in the northeast. The latter has visitor centres, accommodation and self-guided interpretative trails. Durrell Wildlife on Jersey has conducted extensive research on this species. Details at: www.durrellwildlife.org

THREATS

Continuing deforestation means that only around 15% of Cuba's original vegetation cover remains. The solenodon probably once had no natural predators, but that changed with the European colonisation of the West Indies. It is slow and clumsy, with no obvious means of defence, making it easy prey for introduced dogs, cats and mongooses.

=4
EDGE RANK

Aceramarca gracile mouse-opossum

Gracilinanus aceramarcae

Head/body length: approx 70–135mm
Tail length: approx 90–155mm; Weight: 23–34g

Out of pocket

This is not your typical marsupial. For starters it doesn't have a pouch. In keeping with the name, gracile mouse-opossums are small and delicate. They have dense fur that is reddish-brown or greyish-brown above and cream below, with dark eye-rings that look like a pair of spectacles. The tail is slender and usually covered in scales.

This species has been found in tropical cloud forests on the eastern slopes of the Andes at altitudes of 2,600–3,300m. It is known from three areas in La Paz Department, Bolivia, and one similar location in Peru.

Ravenous critter

We know very little about this mouse-opossum. Like most of its kind, it is probably a nocturnal tree dweller, but may venture to the forest floor in search of fruit, insects and other small invertebrates. Its appetite is reputedly voracious.

WHERE TO SEE IT

As little or no research has taken place and no conservation projects are in place, good sites are hard to recommend. The best bet is to search suitable habitat by night in areas close to where known specimens have been found.

THREATS

Habitat destruction from widespread clearing of brush is the main threat. This problem is particularly acute for a species with such a restricted range.

35
EDGE RANK

Short-tailed chinchilla

Chinchilla brevicaudata

Head/body length: 225–380mm
Tail length: 75–150mm; Weight: 400–800g

Famous fur

Chinchillas are the unfortunate victims of their own luxuriant fur, for which they have been hunted for centuries. They are rodents, although their long hind legs and short forelegs make them look more like rabbits. Females are generally larger than males.

This species differs from its cousin, the long-tailed chinchilla by its shorter tail, stockier body and smaller ears. It lives at heights of 3,000–5,000m in the freezing Andes, hence the thick fur. Although its historic range included southern Peru, Bolivia,

northwest Argentina and northern Chile, today it is known only from northern Chile.

Crevice colonies

Chinchilla live in colonies in rocky crevices. They emerge around dusk to forage, feeding on any vegetation they can find. Females produce two or three fully furred young. These are weaned at six to eight weeks and reach sexual maturity by just eight months.

WHERE TO SEE IT

In 2001 a few live specimens were collected in northern Chile. Before then, the last sightings were in the 1970s in Chile's Lauca National Park. Look out for its cousin, the long-tailed chinchilla, at Reserva Nacional Las Chinchillas. Details at: www.wildchinchillas.org

THREATS

This species was brought to the brink of extinction by the fur trade, which began in 1828. Millions of pelts were exported to the West. Illegal trapping persists.

57
EDGE RANK

Maned three-toed sloth

Bradypus torquatus

Head/body length: 45–70cm
Tail length: 5–9 cm
Weight: 2.25–6.2kg

Back garden

If ever an animal coined the phrase 'life in the slow lane' it's a sloth. So slowly do these creatures move that, believe it or not, algae grows on their back. There are six species in all, divided into two groups: three-toed sloths have three toes on each limb; two-toed sloths have two on their forelimbs but three on their hind limbs.

The maned three-toed sloth is the largest and rarest. It gets its name from the mane of black hair that cascades over its shoulders. Otherwise its coat is greyish-brown with a greenish tinge of algae that helps with camouflage. Like all sloths, it has a small round head, a flat face, and long limbs for clambering around the branches. It also has more neck vertebrae than other mammals, allowing it to turn its head through 270 degrees.

This species inhabits lowland tropical rainforest with an unbroken tree canopy. It is restricted to shrinking fragments of Atlantic coastal rainforest in eastern Brazil, especially in the states of Bahia and Espirito Santo.

Hanging around

Sloths spend their entire lives hanging around in trees and sleep for more than 15 hours a day. The only time they descend to the ground is for their weekly comfort break. Here they have to crawl on their soles and forearms and are very vulnerable, though they can defend themselves against predators using their long, sharp claws.

WHERE TO SEE IT

Serra dos Orgaos National Park is a possible site and has good tourist facilities. Una Biological Reserve also has a resident population, and a canopy walkway may improve your chances. The only guaranteed sighting is at the Centre for Zoobotanic Rehabilitation Reserve at Ilhéus, in the south of Bahia. More than 200 maned three-toed sloths have been treated here, and many rehabilitated.

THREATS

This species is especially vulnerable due to its naturally restricted range. The Atlantic coastal rainforest of Brazil is becoming increasingly fragmented due to logging, charcoal production, and clearance for plantations and cattle pasture. This unique habitat now covers less than 10% of its original area.

63
EDGE RANK

One tree can be home to a sloth for long periods. It feeds on young leaves, tender twigs and buds, which it crops with hardened lips rather than teeth. Its rudimentary teeth grow continuously but are worn down equally quickly by the constant grinding of food.

Much like ruminants, sloths have a multi-compartmented stomach filled with cellulose-digesting bacteria. This allows them to extract maximum energy from their nutrient-poor diet. They also have an unusually low metabolic rate, which helps conserve energy.

Individuals can be 'active' both night and day, but rarely travel more than 40m daily. They are primarily solitary, although their home ranges frequently overlap.

Maned three-toed sloths appear to reach maturity at about three years of age. Breeding take place around the end of the dry season (September–November), with females bearing a single young each year. Infants are independent by 11 months.

Maned wolf

Chrysocyon brachyurus

Head/body length: 120–130cm
Height at shoulder: 74–78cm
Tail length: 40–50cm; Weight: 20–23kg

Lanky lupine

This is a rather different wolf from the 'big bad' one of *Little Red Riding Hood* fame that is more familiar to those of us in northern climes. Standing nearly a metre tall on its extremely long, thin legs, it is unmistakable. In fact, you might describe it as resembling a shaggy fox on stilts.

Other very distinctive characteristics of South America's largest wild dog are its long golden-red coat, long pointed muzzle, erect triangular ears, black legs and strip of black hair running from the back of the head to the shoulders. This hair stands erect when the wolf is threatened or alarmed to form the mane after which it is named.

Long grass

The maned wolf lives in tall grasslands, scrubby forest edges and even swampy areas. In Brazil it occurs in the Cerrado, a large area of open woodland and savannah. Its long legs are assumed to be an adaptation to its habitat, enabling it to see over the tall grass.

A wide range covers central South America, from northeastern Brazil, south through Paraguay and west into Peru, including small areas of Argentina and Bolivia. It was once also found in Uraguay but became extinct there during the 19th century.

Fruit forager

The maned wolf forages at night and rests during the day. It hunts a variety of small prey, including pacas, rabbits, small rodents, armadillos and birds, and will occasionally also take fish, reptiles, insects and other invertebrates. But more than 60% of its diet consists of fruit, in particular the tomato-like lobeira fruit, which grows throughout the wolf's range and is known locally as *fruta do lobo* or 'wolf's fruit'.

Unlike its better-known pack cousins, this wolf leads a relatively solitary life. Males and females form stable pairs that share a home range of 25–30 km², but each individual remains fairly independent and they only associate for any length of time during the breeding season between April and June.

A female gives birth to anything from one to five pups each year. While their care and upbringing is predominantly her responsibility, there is some evidence to suggest males also play a role that includes regurgitating food for his offspring. Pups reach sexual maturity and disperse from their natal home range at around one year old, but do not breed until their second year.

WHERE TO SEE IT

You will need to time your trip for the end of the dry season when natural fires reduce the height of long grass and wolves become easier to see. Emas National Park in Brazil and Ibera Marshes Nature Reserve in Argentina are two good places to visit, and both have lots of other wildlife to see as well. Perhaps the most intriguing location is Parque Natural do Caraca in Brazil, where a guesthouse, Hospedaria do Colegio Caraca (once an old monastery), puts out food and has maned wolves visit most nights.

THREATS

Hunting and habitat loss constitute the major threats. Local people attribute mystical qualities to various parts of the wolf's anatomy (eyes, skin, tail) and so still hunt them for these. Sport hunting also continues, and wolves may be persecuted for pestering poultry and other farm stock. Huge areas of habitat have been lost to cattle ranches, and ever-expanding farms have forced the wolf into more likely conflict with humans. Around protected areas they may also fall victim to road traffic, which accounts for up to 50% of pup mortality in some reserves.

No ranking
EDGE RANK

Baird's tapir

Tapirus bairdii

Head/body length: 180–250cm
Height at shoulder: 73–20 cm
Tail length: 5–13cm; Weight: 200–350kg

Truncated trunk

Tapirs look like a halfway house between rhinos and elephants and, with an ancestry that dates back 55 million years, are effectively living fossils. Baird's tapir is the largest indigenous mammal in Central America. Its most distinctive feature is its fleshy, flexible snout, which resembles a shortened version of an elephant's trunk.

Tapirs have stocky, rotund bodies and short powerful legs ideal for dashing through undergrowth. They support their weight on three splayed toes on the back feet and four on the front. Adult are dark brown or grey and covered in sparse bristly hairs. Youngsters, however, have reddish-brown coats marked with stripes and spots like humbug sweets. These markings fade with age.

WHERE TO SEE IT

This species is highly elusive throughout its range. Corcovado National Park in Costa Rica is your best bet, though tracks are easier to see than the animal itself. In the vicinity of Sirenca Biological Station tapirs sometimes visit the beach area to obtain salts and minerals from the ocean.

Details at: http://savetapirs.org;
www.tapirback.com/tapirgal

THREATS

Around 70% of Central American forest has been lost over the last 40 years. Much of this species' habitat is being cleared for ranching and development. Almost all rainforest has vanished in El Salvador and the species is now believed to be extinct there. Tapirs are also hunted for food and sport.

34
EDGE RANK

The tapir family is oddly distributed: one species is found in Southeast Asia and three in Latin America. Baird's tapir was once abundant throughout Central America, from southeast Mexico to northwest Colombia. It has now disappeared from many areas and survives only in forest pockets in Colombia, Ecuador, Costa Rica, Guatemala, Honduras, Mexico, Nicaragua and Panama. It can tolerate a wide variety of habitats, including tropical rainforest, woodland, grassland and marshes, as long as there is a permanent water supply.

Water baby

Tapirs are shy and reclusive. They tend to hide away in thickets by day and emerge at night to browse in forest clearings. Although very short-sighted, their acute sense of smell and excellent hearing help them detect food and danger.

Each day Baird's tapirs eat a large quantity of leaves, twigs, fruit and seeds, using micro-organisms in their gut to help digest plant material. Water is hugely important, and they follow regular trails between favourite pools and streams. Tapirs are capable swimmers and frequently wallow during the day, sometimes evading predators, such as jaguars by diving under water.

This species is thought to live alone or in small family groups, and maintains overlapping home ranges. Individuals may congregate at saltlicks, especially during the mating season. Births occur all year, with the females giving birth to a single (or occasionally two) young. The youngsters stay with their mother for up to two years.

Mountain tapir

Tapirus pinchaque

Head/body length: 180–250cm
Height at shoulder: 70–120cm
Tail length: 5–13cm; Weight: 150–320kg

Woolly jumper

The mountain tapir needs its own built-in fleece for insulation against freezing Andean nights. Its dark reddish-brown or black coat is thus very dense, which explains its alternative name of 'woolly tapir'. It is the smallest tapir species, and has the characteristic flexible snout and bold patterning in juveniles.

Home is the cloud forests and páramo grasslands of the high Andes at altitudes of 2,000–4,300m. Today it is restricted to mountainous parts of Colombia, Ecuador and northern Peru.

Dung dispersal

Remarkable agility allows this large animal to climb steep mountain slopes and even glaciers. It is most active at dawn and dusk, feeding on a various leaves, seeds and shoots, and helping disperse many Andean plant seeds through its droppings.

Pairs or small family groups maintain overlapping home ranges and sometimes congregate at saltlicks. They communicate by urinating on paths and through their shrill whistling call.

WHERE TO SEE IT

Try Ecuador's Sangay National Park, which has a tourist centre with trails and accommodation.

Details at: www.tapirback.com/tapirgal; www.andeantapirfund.com

THREATS

Habitat is being lost to agriculture, while settlements break up populations. Illegal hunting continues for meat, pelts and body parts – the latter used in traditional medicine.

80
EDGE RANK

Monito del monte

Dromiciops gliroides

Head/body length: 80–130mm
Tail length: 90–130mm; Weight: approx 16–42g

Getting a grip

Despite its name, which means 'mountain monkey', this is actually a pocket-sized marsupial that can grip branches with its prehensile tail. It has soft brown fur with greyish-white patches, short tufted ears, and black rings around the eyes.

Prime habitat is cool, humid forests, especially with thickets of Chilean bamboo. It ranges from south-central Chile into the adjoining provinces of Neuquen and Rio Negro in Argentina.

Big sleep

This consummate tree dweller sleeps by day in a small nest of sticks and bamboo leaves lined with

grass and moss. At night it forages for insects, other invertebrates and occasionally fruit.

In winter it hibernates, sustained by fat reserves in its tail. Pairs join up during the mating season (October–December). The young at first ride in their mother's pouch; later they transfer to her back.

WHERE TO SEE IT

This species has recently been found in Chile's Valdivian Coastal Reserve. Scientists are also studying it on the island of Chiloé. Find out about volunteer placements at: www.worldwildlife.org/travel; www.sendadarwin.cl

THREATS

Outside protected areas this species is threatened by habitat loss, as well as competition and predation from introduced black rats. Local superstitions hold that it brings bad luck if found in a home.

42
EDGE RANK

Volcano rabbit
Romerolagus diazi

Head/body length: 270–315mm
Ear length: 40–44mm; **Weight:** 385–600g

Baby bunny
This is possibly the world's smallest rabbit, and has a stubby nose, short ears, short legs and virtually no tail. Its dense dark brown or black fur is flecked yellow on the upper parts.

Volcano rabbits live in open pine forests and secondary alder forests with dense undergrowth at elevations of 2,800–4,250m. Most areas suffer winter droughts, but have plentiful summer rains. Endemic to central Mexico, they are found on the slopes of just four volcanoes: Popocatepetl and Iztaccihuatl (Sierra Nevada); and El Pelado and Tlaloc (Sierra Chichinautzin).

Tunnel trails
This mainly nocturnal species is most active just before dawn or after dusk, using well-maintained runways through the undergrowth. It lives in groups of two to five in areas of bunch grass called *zacaton*. While it may sometimes use old burrows, it more often hides in the grass.

WHERE TO SEE IT
A serious challenge. The best place is Izta-Popo National Park, and around the volcanoes Popocatepetl and Iztaccihuatl. There is accommodation at Altzomoni lodge. Register at: http://iztapopo.conanp.gob.mx

THREATS
This little-known rabbit has recently disappeared from some areas due to habitat destruction and hunting. Problems also include forest fires and over-grazing.

41 EDGE RANK

Chacoan peccary
Catagonus wagneri

Head/body length: 90–110cm
Height at shoulder: 52–69cm
Tail length: 2.5–10cm; **Weight:** 30–40kg

Pretend porker
Peccaries look just like pigs, with their long, flexible snout and bristly coat, but they actually belong to a separate New World family. Differences include their longer, more slender legs, and their smaller, downward-pointing canines. They also have a mane of stiff dark hairs along the back and a faint whitish collar that extends to the shoulders.

The Chacoan peccary is the largest and rarest of three species. It lives in hot, semi-arid thorn forests and steppe, dominated by low-lying succulent plants and thorny bushes. It is endemic to the Gran Chaco region of western Paraguay, southeastern Bolivia and northern Argentina, where its distribution is patchy.

Water retention
Chacoan peccaries are well adapted to their dry environment: they get moisture from the fleshy plants that dominate their diet, and have efficient kidneys that retain as much water as possible. Groups of up to ten wander home ranges of around 1,000ha. They can live for up to nine years.

WHERE TO SEE IT
Parque Nacional Defensores del Chaco, Paraguay's largest park, is hard to reach but offers the best chance of finding wild Chacoan peccaries. In Argentina, El Copo Provincial reserve, in Santiago del Estero Province, is the only protected area with Chacoan peccaries.

THREATS
The loss of habitat and its conversion to cattle pasture is a serious threat. Illegal hunting for meat, even within protected areas, has also had a heavy impact on populations.

67 EDGE RANK

Spectacled bear

Tremarctos ornatus

Head/body length: 130–200cm
Height at shoulder: 70–90cm
Weight: 100–175kg (males); 60–80kg (females)

WHERE TO SEE IT

Sightings are more a matter of luck than planning. Parque Nacional Podocarpus and Parque Nacional Sangay in Ecuador both have good trails to walk and apparently the bears can be heard howling at night from local lodges. Parque Nacional Amboro in Bolivia also has a reasonable record of sightings, as does Parque Nacional Los Nevados in Colombia. But nowhere are there any guarantees. Alternatively you can volunteer to radio-track spectacled bears in the wild: a research project based in the Intag Region of northern Ecuador and led by ecologist and bear expert Armando Castellanos offers this opportunity. Details at: www.andeanbear.org

THREATS

Habitat destruction is inevitably the major cause of decline for this species. Local farmers also persecute bears, blaming them for killing cattle and destroying maize crops. Hunting for meat, skin, fat, claws and other body parts continues to be a concern, with the gall bladders being sold to traditional oriental medicine markets.

178
EDGE RANK

Pretend panda

Looking at a spectacled bear, you don't need too much imagination to see that its closest living relative is a giant panda. And after the panda, it is the most endangered bear.

This species is relatively small, with dense black or dark brown fur. It has a distinctive and variable pattern of white or creamy facial markings, which sometimes form the 'spectacle' pattern around the eyes from which the bear derives its name. These markings also continue onto the chest, and their arrangement is unique to each individual.

High mountain home

Spectacled bears, also known as Andean bears, occur in a wide range of habitats throughout the Andean mountain range, including montane forest, cloud forest, high altitude grasslands and scrub desert. They prefer elevations above 2,000m and may even venture near the snowline at 4,700m. Their range extends through the Andes from Venezuela to northern Argentina.

Seed spreader

This little-known bear is the largest carnivore in South America. Like other bears it is probably a diurnal omnivore. It is also a good climber.

Plant matter forms the bulk of its diet, especially bromeliads, but also bamboo, fruits and cactuses. Consequently it plays an important role in spreading a variety of seeds through its droppings. Locals sometimes accuse spectacled bears of killing cattle, but most such instances involve bears seen scavenging on animals that are already dead.

A shocking discovery

Andrew Evans

The New World has always represented new discoveries. When the explorer Alexander Von Humboldt (1769–1859) ventured up the Orinoco River, he took a hands-on approach to wildlife and picked up a strange green fish in the shallows. He was immediately knocked to the ground by the powerful shock of the electric eel (*Electrophorus electricus*), the first electrical animal ever documented. In the name of research, Humboldt shocked himself again and again before asking his travel partner to do the same, 'as a test'.

▲ Alexander von Humboldt (centre) with Schiller, Wilhelm and Goethe (Painting by Adolph Müller)

The indigenous American peoples had already benefited from several thousand years of their own discoveries. Their livelihood depended upon understanding the species around them, such as the seemingly limitless bison. They also passed on a generational memory of prehistoric 'megafauna', such as mammoths. Much of the work of European naturalists was simply putting this native knowledge into print. The 1536 expedition of French explorer Jacques Cartier, for instance, was saved by annedda, a new tree pointed out by Domagaya, the son of a local Iroquois chief, and now known as the Northern White Cedar (*Thuja occidentalis*). The vitamin C extracted from boiling its needles cured the scurvy of 85 French sailors.

Greater than gold

Ounce for ounce, cinnamon was worth more than gold in 16th century Spain. While his brother Francisco was busy conquering the Aztecs, Gonzalo Pizarro went looking for both these riches in the fabled city of gold, 'El Dorado', and the equally enchanted 'land of cinnamon' (though cinnamon is actually indigenous to southern Asia). The 1541 expedition over the Ecuadorian Andes was a complete disaster that left thousands of natives dead and a small party stranded on the other side of the mountains. Unable to return upstream, Francisco de Orellana and his team sailed down one river and then the next, following each tributary with awe as the great river revealed itself. Among his fantastical tales, Orellana told of fierce female warriors, or *Amazonas*. The name stuck, and South America's longest river has intrigued travellers ever since.

▲ Charles Rath, famous buffalo hunter, seated on 40,000 buffalo hides in Robert Wright's Dodge City hide yard in 1878

The search for new plants also opened up new areas for discovery: sugar, coffee, cocoa and tobacco each sparked a curiosity about tropical ecology. Business ventures invariably turned into natural history expeditions. Such was the mission of the Lewis and Clark expedition (1804–06), who were dispatched to grasp some inkling of what lay inside the recent Louisiana Purchase. The Shoshone woman Sacagawea guided the team to the Pacific Ocean, helping them name and record 120 animal and 200 plant species. About halfway through his journey, William Clark noted that he would stop writing about the thousands of bison, caribou and antelope that he saw because readers would surely think it all an exaggeration.

The President's pet

Lewis and Clark made constant attempts to capture souvenirs of their expedition. Grizzly bears proved too dangerous, but the explorers had more luck with a colony of 'barking squirrels', an apt description for the black-tailed prairie dog (*Cynomys ludovicianus*). They finally caught a small pup and the little animal endured a four-month journey in a crate, first by barge down the Mississippi, then by ship to Washington, DC, where he was presented as a gift to Thomas Jefferson. The president described him as a 'most harmless and tame creature' and kept him as a pet in the White House for four years.

▲ Lewis and Clark on the Lower Columbia (painting by Charles Marion Russell)

Andrew Evans is a freelance travel writer based in Washington, DC. A native of Texas, he is the author of the Bradt Guides to Ukraine, Kiev, and Iceland.

Background: Pack train in Sierra Nevada, California, by Ansel Adams, c.1934

The American writer Henry David Thoreau (1817–62) took a less acquisitive approach, choosing instead to entertain readers with longhand accounts of his quiet life on the shores of Walden Pond. His book *Walden* became a bible for Transcendentalists who believed that nature and spirit were invariably connected. Today, Thoreau is considered America's great home-grown hero and *Walden* is required reading in schools. Meanwhile Scottish immigrant John Muir (1838–1914) dropped out of university to pursue 'wilderness' and found it by walking on foot from Indiana to Florida. The rugged outdoorsman ended up in California where he fell in love with the landscapes of Yosemite. While others focused on finding gold, Muir gave value to America's wilderness by describing it in rich emotional detail. His prolific writing would set the foundation of the later conservation movement.

Thus depicting wildlife became as vital as wildlife itself. The first guide to North American flora and fauna was published by English naturalist Mark Catesby (1683–1749), whose *Natural History of Carolina, Florida, and the Bahamas* served as the reference on new world species for taxonomist Carl Linnaeus. John James Audubon (1785–1851), born in Haiti, spent half his life painting life-sized colour portraits of birds in their natural habitat. His book *Birds of America* became the categorical standard for natural historians; a recent auction of an original copy gained the highest price ever paid for a single book. Likewise, photographer Ansel Adams (1902–84) captured iconic black-and-white images of America's national parks and forests, some of which were chosen by NASA to travel on board the *Voyager* spacecraft as examples of life on Earth. Until such expeditions discover worlds beyond our own, the Americas still represent our greatest scope for discovery.

▲ Greater flamingo, from Audubon's Birds of America.

Giant armadillo

Priodontes maximus

Head/body length: 50–70cm
Tail length: 40–60cm; **Weight:** 18–32kg

Shell suit

Armadillos are amongst the oldest and oddest mammals, trundling along in a suit of armour that wouldn't look out of place on a medieval knight. This 'shell' actually consists of bony plates or 'scutes', overlaid with horny skin.

The giant armadillo is the largest species, with 11–13 hinged plates protecting its body and three or four more on the neck. It has a pale head and long front claws. However, it is puny compared with its extinct relatives: some weighed over 1,000kg and early indigenous peoples used their shells as roofs!

Giant armadillos live in undisturbed wet tropical forest, plus adjacent grassland and bush, and prefer areas near water. Their range extends east of the Andes, from north Venezuela through Brazil to Paraguay and north Argentina.

Armour-plated insect-eater

This species is solitary and nocturnal, spending the day sheltering in burrows. Unlike its smaller cousins, it can't roll into a ball for protection so also uses these burrows to escape predators. The powerful legs and massive front claws rip open termite mounds to get at termites. Other food includes ants, spiders and worms.

WHERE TO SEE IT

Seeing this shy animal is a challenge. Emas National Park in Brazil's Pantanal offers a chance and night drives can prove fruitful. Responsible Travel offers Conservation Projects in Emas. Details at: www.responsibletravel.com

THREATS

Giant armadillos are hunted for food, which may have depleted the population by up to 50% in the last ten years. Habitat loss is also a serious factor.

203
EDGE RANK

Andean cat

Oreailurus jacobita

Head/body length: approx 60–70cm
Height at shoulder: approx 30cm
Tail length: approx 40–50cm; **Weight:** approx 3.5–6kg

Mountain miniature

Looking a bit like a miniature snow leopard, the Andean cat is one of the most endangered wild cats in the world. It is small but sturdy, with luxuriant fur to protect it from the bitter cold of its mountain home. Its ash-grey body

is marked with spots, stripes and bars, while its banded tail is long and thick.

Regarded as sacred in some Andean cultures, the Andean cat lives in rocky and arid areas above 4,000m in the high Andes. It is sparsely distributed across Argentina, Bolivia, Chile and Peru.

Mystery moggy

One of the world's least-known cats. Sightings do occur by day, but it is probably more active around dusk and at night. It is thought to be mainly solitary, and to use its acute sense of hearing to help capture prey, which includes rodents – notably the mountain viscacha – and small birds.

WHERE TO SEE IT

Its remote, challenging habitat makes this a very difficult species to see. You will need to be fit – and very lucky. Recent sightings have been in Campode los Alisos National Park in Argentina and Sajama National Park in Bolivia. Details at: www.wildnet.org/andean_cat.htm

THREATS

This cat naturally occurs at low densities. Indigenous Andean peoples have long hunted it, using its pelt in traditional ceremonies. The decline of chinchilla populations (see page 124), once a major prey item, has probably also affected it severely.

No ranking
EDGE RANK

Brazilian three-banded armadillo

Tolypeutes tricinctus

Head/body length: 22–27cm
Tail length: 6–8cm; Weight: 1.0–1.6kg

Having a ball

This endearing little creature has the handy knack of being able to turn itself into an impregnable, pocket-sized fortress. It is the only armadillo able completely to enclose itself in its own shell by rolling into a ball – about the size of a large melon. The front and rear portions of the shell hang down freely like a skirt, allowing it to tuck its head, legs and tail into the space inside when it rolls up.

There are two species of three-banded armadillo, the Brazilian and the southern, with the former being far more endangered. Both have a blackish-brown shell with flexible bands across the back that allow it to articulate. Most individuals have three bands, but others may have two or four. These animals generally walk on the tips of the foreclaws, even when running.

The Brazilian three-banded armadillo prefers dry habitats, frequenting thorny scrub forests (*caatinga*) and bush grassland (*cerrado*) in northeastern and central Brazil. It is now restricted to parts of the northern highlands, including the provinces of Pernambuco, Piauí, Maranhão, western Bahia and northern Minas Gerais.

Shut your trap

Three-banded armadillos are generally solitary, but groups of up to 12 may share a den during cold spells. They feed on ants, termites and beetle larvae, as well as fruits – especially during the wet season. Strong claws help them to excavate insects and grubs from mounds or rotting wood.

Rolling into a tight ball provides a defence against natural enemies. If harassed further, they begin to open up partially and then snap shut again like a gin-trap to try and scare off their attacker.

A single young is born between November and January. It is fully formed, resembling a miniature version of its parents, and can walk and roll into a ball immediately.

WHERE TO SEE IT

There have been some sightings in Grande Sertao Veredas National Park in northern Minas Gerais (on the border between Minas Gerais and Bahia states). You also have a good chance of seeing this elusive creature in Amacayacu National Park, which offers good facilities, including a research and visitor centre and overnight accommodation within the reserve.

Brazil

THREATS

This species is easily captured for food. Its naturally fragmented habitat is now threatened by agriculture, and felling trees for charcoal and mining. Populations have dropped by over 30% in the last decade and it has already disappeared from much of its range. Densities remain very low.

292
EDGE RANK

American bison

Bison bison

Head/body length: 2.1–3.5m
Height at shoulder: 1.5–1.8m
Tail length: 30–60cm
Weight: 350–1000kg

Slaughter

Perhaps more than any other mammal, the history of the bison illustrates the devastating effect our species can have on the natural world. Herds millions-strong once swept across the great plains of North America. By 1900, after a deliberate and wholesale slaughter, fewer than 1,000 remained.

The cultures of numerous indigenous peoples, from Comanche to Kiowa, had long revolved around the bison. They depended on its meat for food, and its hides for clothing and shelter. The arrival of the railroad in the mid-19th century and the movement west of European settlers changed this forever. These newcomers set out to remove the indigenous peoples and make way for their cattle by massacring the bison. Three million were shot in 1872–74 alone.

The American bison is the largest terrestrial mammal in the New World. Its top-heavy build, with massive forequarters and head, is unmistakable. During winter it grows a shaggy brown coat that is particularly thick and dark on its withers, neck and head. Both sexes have short, curved horns, which they use in fights.

Gulf to Rockies

The American bison lives in open grasslands, aspen parkland and coniferous forest. Although associated with the western prairies, it once ranged right across North America from the Gulf of Mexico to the Great Lakes and up through the Rockies into Canada. Today free-ranging animals are confined to various parks and wildlife refuges. Many originate from semi-domestic stock and the only continuously wild herd is in Yellowstone National Park, Wyoming, which now numbers around 3,000 and is descended from a remnant population of just 23. Bison are now also reared for meat: there are at least a quarter of a million on commercial ranches.

Seasonal wanderer

Bison are highly gregarious animals and outside the breeding season only mature bulls live alone. The rut begins in July, when males establish dominance by posturing and fighting – although in any one year only around 35% get to breed. Most mating occurs in August and September, with a single tan calf born the following spring.

Bison graze on grasses and sedges, and are hugely important in maintaining healthy grassland ecosystems. The continuous application of their dung and urine results in grazed pasture producing up to 80% more grass than ungrazed pasture. Herds are nomadic, following good grazing. In Yellowstone, they move to high-altitude grassland in summer, where the grazing is rich and nutritious, but are forced lower down in winter by bad weather and deep snow.

Despite their bulk, bison can jump up to 1.8m high and reach 55 km/h. They are too big for most predators, though wolves and grizzly bears take calves, and occasionally old or weakened adults. Sexual maturity comes at three years of age and they live for 18–22 years in the wild.

WHERE TO SEE IT

There are numerous places in North America and Canada to see semi-domesticated and reintroduced bison. However, the best places for genuine wild animals are Yellowstone and Grand Teton National Parks in Wyoming, both of which encapsulate the grandeur of the American West. In Yellowstone large herds are often seen in the Lamar River valley and along the banks of the Firehole River. In the winter this area has an ethereal feel, as bison wander through deep snow against a backdrop of steaming geysers.

THREATS

A concerted effort since the turn of the 20th century, including extensive breeding and reintroduction programmes, has saved this species from extinction. However, conflicts still remain. As numbers in Yellowstone have grown, bison have moved out of the park, particularly in winter, and have met fierce resistance from local ranchers – primarily because they carry a cattle disease (brucellosis) that would spell economic disaster if it spread to livestock. The authorities culled over 1,000 bison around Yellowstone in the severe winter of 1996–97. There is now a plan to vaccinate bison and minimise future conflicts.

No ranking
EDGE RANK

Amazonian manatee

Trichechus inunguis

Head/tail length: 2.5–3m; Weight: 350–500kg

WHERE TO SEE IT

In Brazil you can see Amazonian manatees in Parque Nacional Amacayacu. Your best bet is to visit between April and August when local guides take you to the oxbow lakes and waterways where manatees might be found. In Venezuela boat trips through the mangroves of the Orinoco Delta also offer a good chance, while in Ecuador manatees are occasionally seen in lakes in Yasuni National Park. Details at: www.jakera.com; http://orinocodelta.com; www.sanilodge.com

THREATS

Slow-moving manatees are easy targets and have been widely hunted throughout their range for their meat, oil, fat and hides. Commercial hunting, which began in the 17th century, has devastated populations in many areas. This industry peaked in the 1950s, with some 4,000–10,000 manatees killed annually in Brazil alone. Hunting is now illegal, but threats remain, including accidental drowning in fishing nets, and the silting of waterways from soil erosion caused by deforestation

84
EDGE RANK

No fluke

Manatees are peculiar, torpedo-shaped aquatic mammals that look like a curious combination of whale and hippo. They are characterised by their rotund body, small head and squarish mouth. The split upper lip is covered with thick bristles and each half can move independently. The tail is round and paddle-shaped, rather than fluked and whale-like as in the similar dugong.

The Amazonian manatee is smaller and more slender than other manatees. Its flippers are also longer, and its skin smoother and more rubbery. It inhabits lagoons, oxbows and backwater lakes with abundant aquatic vegetation and connecting channels to large rivers. Its range covers the Amazon Basin, from the river mouth to the upper tributaries in Brazil, Guyana, Columbia, Peru and Ecuador. It may overlap with the West Indian manatee along the Brazilian coast.

High and low water

Amazonian manatees often feed at the surface, where they resemble giant floating sausages. They are shy and secretive, and only their nostrils protrude above water. Their herbivorous diet comprises a variety of aquatic vegetation, including grasses, water lettuce and water hyacinths. This is low-quality food, so they must eat the equivalent of 8–15% of their body weight daily.

These slow-moving creatures live individually or in small groups, with mothers and calves always travelling together. Larger herds were once known to assemble in the middle reaches of the Amazon.

Manatees make seasonal movements to coincide with the rise and fall of floodwaters. When levels are high they move into flooded forest where feeding is good. But when the waters recede they sometimes become trapped in larger lakes and have to remain there until the waters return. At such times food becomes scare and they may have to live on their fat reserves. They can survive seven months without eating.

The gestation period is 13 months. Females give birth only every three or four years. They nurse their calves from a teat behind the flipper, and calves remain dependent for a considerable period.

Giant river otter

Pteronura brasiliensis

Head/body length: 95–125cm
Tail length: 45–85cm
Weight: 22–32kg

WHERE TO SEE IT

Brazil

Densities being low, this species is hard to see. Sightings depend upon water levels. Two places offer a reasonable chance: at Rio Pixaim in Brazil's Pantanal you can see habituated otters at close quarters from boats (stay at the Hotel Beira Rio); at Guyana's Iwokrama Forest Reserve you can take a guided canoe trip down the Rupununi River to Karanambu to see both wild otters and an otter rehabilitation project. Details at: www.andeantrails.co.uk/guyanawildlife.htm; iwokrama@guyana.net.gy

THREATS

Giant otters have no natural predators and numbers are primarily decreasing due to human pressures. In the past they were excessively hunted for their valuable fur, and hunting persists today despite being illegal. But habitat loss and pollution constitute greater threats, especially when mining run-off pollutes river systems. Otters are also sometimes accidentally trapped in fishing nets.

No ranking
EDGE RANK

River wolf

Known locally as 'river wolf', this super-slinky customer is one of South America's top predators and the world's rarest otter. It has large webbed feet to propel it through the water, a long tail that acts like a rudder and a sinuous body covered in velvety, water-repellent fur. The brown pelt has a creamy pattern on the throat and chin that is unique in each individual.

This otter prefers slow-moving rivers, lakes and backwaters, with gently sloping banks and plenty of overhanging vegetation. Its range includes every South American country except Argentina, Uruguay and Chile, and encompasses the entire the Orinoco, Amazon and La Plata river systems.

Amphibious assassin

Giant otters are social animals. Groups comprise breeding pairs and their offspring. Each occupies a riverside territory and spends the night in large, communal dens constructed under fallen logs or behind root systems. They also use striking communal latrines, clearing and scent marking an area of up to 50m². The area is stripped of vegetation and left stinking of otter, leaving a pungent advertisement of the family's presence.

Giant otters are strictly diurnal. They are rather cumbersome on land – although able to travel considerable distances – but in the water are transformed into swift, dynamic hunters. They hunt alone or as a pack, and have the agility to capture a wide variety of fish. Their large eyes and sensitive whiskers help them detect prey in murky water, which they then usually eat at the surface.

Breeding takes place throughout the year, although young are usually born between August and October. Litter size varies from one to five cubs (or 'kits'). The whole family helps care for them and they remain hidden in the den for two to three weeks. Youngsters become fully independent at nine months and remain with their family group until sexual maturity at two years or more.

Conserving wildlife in the New World

The large-scale arrival of Europeans and Africans in the Americas after 1500 brought about a massive population crash among the indigenous peoples, who quickly succumbed to diseases brought over by the new colonisers. Much of the indigenous wildlife has also suffered significant losses as a direct or indirect result of this colonisation and, while the species composition in the New World is very different from that of the Old, there are many parallels to be drawn in conservation terms.

Hunted out

North America was once home to both the world's most numerous bird and most numerous large mammal. At the start of the 19th century there were thought to be 40 million American bison ranging from northern Canada to Mexico with, at the same time, an estimated five billion passenger pigeons in the United States alone. While both species must then have seemed to represent an inexhaustible resource, hunting on a massive scale devastated their populations in a shockingly short time, leaving both close to extinction by the end of the century. For the pigeon, which became extinct in the early 1900s, it was too late. The bison was saved only by a concerted conservation effort and today the Buffalo Field Campaign (*www.buffalofieldcampaign.org*) is an organisation driven by voluntary workers that works to protect Yellowstone Park's remaining bison.

These cautionary tales have not gone unheeded and, while hunting for food and fun remains a popular pursuit in North America today, it is strictly regulated and often tied into wildlife management practice. For example, since 1934 wildfowl hunters have been obliged to purchase Federal Duck Stamps (*www.fws.gov/duckstamps*), which both serve as hunting licences and generate revenue towards the purchase and protection of wetlands.

Forests across the New World are equally in need of protection. Commercial logging has heavily depleted both the boreal forests of northern Canada, and the tropical rainforests of Central and South America. Canada has a tenth of the world's forest cover, but less than 8% of this land is fully protected and the remainder is fast being fragmented and destroyed, threatening entire ecosystems. Global Forest Watch (*www.globalforestwatch.org*) is involved in publicising this situation and campaigning for improved forest management. Meanwhile Brazil, the world's most biodiverse country with an astounding 524 species of mammal and 17% of global forest cover, is losing a shocking 17,600km^2 of virgin forest each year. Imazon (*www.imazon.org.br/imazon/index.asp*) is researching ways in which to manage the remaining rainforests sustainably.

Cutting edge: Only a tiny proportion of Canada's pine forest is protected from commercial logging. ▲

Island states

Evolution on small islands takes place in a microcosm. With a small founder population of animals and very specific natural selection pressures, the species that evolve may be quite different from those that occupy similar niches on the mainland. These island endemics, adapted to a particular set of conditions and often existing in small numbers, are extremely vulnerable to changes in their habitat, especially hunting and the introduction of more adaptable species from the mainland. In the Americas, the shrew-like solenodons of Cuba and Hispaniola are the sole representatives of their family, and both face extinction thanks to the introduction of cats and mongooses to their islands. Island Conservation (www.islandconservation.org) is an organisation dedicated to researching and protecting endemic island animals in North America.

Something fishy: Salmon farming in Chile causes serious sea pollution – the WWF is working to discourage the practice. ▶

Fighting development

The countries of South America are changing fast, eager to catch up economically with their northern neighbours. This has had an inevitable impact upon their indigenous people, wildlife and wild places. For example, large-scale infrastructure projects such as highway building in Chile threaten the only temperate rainforest in South America, in the country's southern Valdivia region. The World Wildlife Fund (*www.wwf.org*) has designated this area as one of its Priority Places. Other threats to the region

include deforestation (60% of the forest cover is already gone), while the growing salmon farming industry in the Patagonian lakes threatens native fishes and is polluting sea waters which host, among other species, the endangered blue whale. WWF's efforts to protect the region have already led the world's largest salmon farming company to withdraw its lake operations, and it is now working with forestry companies to develop new sustainable forest management strategies.

Another WWF project centres upon the Chihuahuan Desert in Mexico. This is the world's most biodiverse desert and is home to 3,500 plant species, including 1,000 regional endemics, as well as the endangered Mexican prairie dog and deer mouse. As with natural deserts everywhere, its ecological importance is under appreciated, and overgrazing and the misuse of water supplies are seriously damaging its exceptional natural riches. The WWF's work focuses on educating the local community in sustainable development, especially helping farmers with water management, as well as identifying the most important areas for biodiversity protection schemes.

Island invasion

Observations in the Galápagos helped Charles Darwin formulate his theories on evolution, and the archipelago's significance in the natural world cannot be overstated. However, despite their remoteness – lying 1,000km off Ecuador in the Pacific Ocean – the islands have suffered at the hand of man: sailors killed giant tortoises and introduced goats, rats and other species that have devastated much native fauna and flora. Conservationists continue to fight to reduce this impact and have been successful in repatriating tortoises to many islands. Paradoxically, the popularity of the islands is also a cause for concern, as the burgeoning ecotourism industry has led to unsustainable local development.

Snap happy: Marine iguanas and other unique animals draw increasing numbers of tourists to the Galápagos ▶

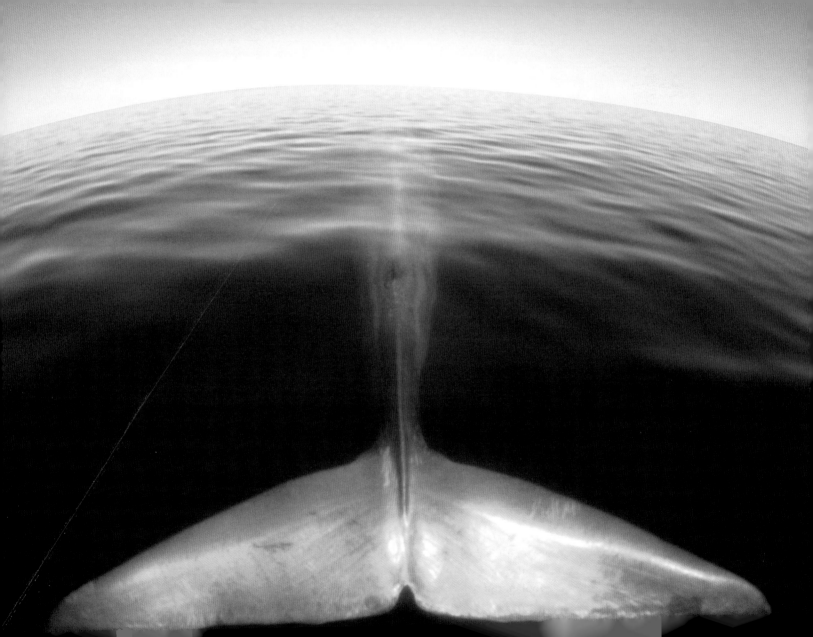

Oceans

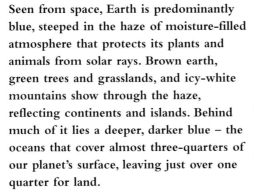

Seen from space, Earth is predominantly blue, steeped in the haze of moisture-filled atmosphere that protects its plants and animals from solar rays. Brown earth, green trees and grasslands, and icy-white mountains show through the haze, reflecting continents and islands. Behind much of it lies a deeper, darker blue – the oceans that cover almost three-quarters of our planet's surface, leaving just over one quarter for land.

From a biological point of view this huge region can be divided neatly into two: the shallow seas above the continental shelf and the deep open oceans beyond them. In the shallow seas water is rarely deeper than 200m, and the seabed is generally covered in rich sediments of sand and mud. From a biodiversity perspective these are the richest regions of the ocean. Contrast this with the deep open oceans where the seabed plummets to several kilometres (at its deepest point, in the Marianas Trench, the ocean floor is 10,923m below the surface), plunging everything into complete darkness. These depths are a strange world that remains as alien to us as the surface of Mars.

Yet in the upper layers where light remains the open oceans are remarkable productive. Here plant plankton or phytoplankton (mainly algae) flourishes in vast quantities. It fuels the great ocean food webs, and produces probably half the mass of the world's living matter while releasing half the atmosphere's oxygen. In turn, this thick nutrient soup supports enormous quantities of zooplankton, which ranges from tiny single-celled creatures to small crustaceans such as krill that provide food for the largest animals ever to live, the great whales.

◀ *The tail flukes of a blue whale, unlike those of many of its relatives, seldom break the surface before it dives.*

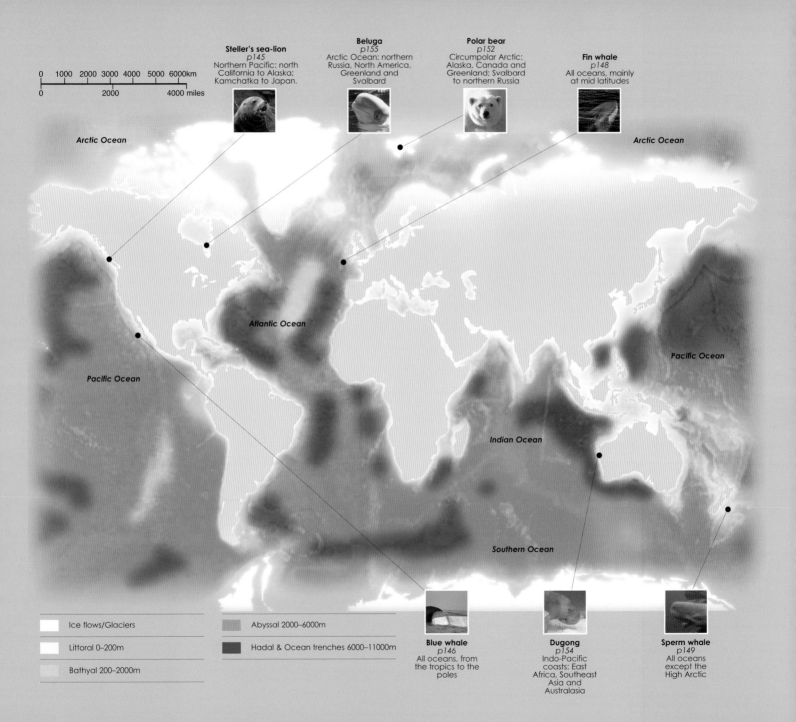

Steller's sea-lion
p145
Northern Pacific: north
California to Alaska;
Kamchatka to Japan.

Beluga
p155
Arctic Ocean: northern
Russia, North America,
Greenland and
Svalbard

Polar bear
p152
Circumpolar Arctic:
Alaska, Canada and
Greenland; Svalbard
to northern Russia

Fin whale
p148
All oceans, mainly
at mid latitudes

Arctic Ocean

Arctic Ocean

0   1000 2000 3000 4000 5000 6000km

0   2000   4000 miles

Atlantic Ocean

Pacific Ocean

Pacific Ocean

Indian Ocean

Southern Ocean

Blue whale
p146
All oceans, from
the tropics to the
poles

Dugong
p154
Indo-Pacific
coasts: East
Africa, Southeast
Asia and
Australasia

Sperm whale
p149
All oceans
except the
High Arctic

Ice flows/Glaciers

Littoral 0–200m

Bathyal 200–2000m

Abyssal 2000–6000m

Hadal & Ocean trenches 6000–11000m

Steller's sealion

Eumetopias jubatus

**Head/body length: up to 3m (males);
up to 2.3m (females)
Weight: up to 700kg (males); up to 300kg (females)**

Cool-water customers

Sea-lions get their name from the long, coarse mane of the thick-necked males, and differ from regular seals in having visible ears. Steller's sea-lion is the largest species. Bulls (males) are twice the size of cows (females). Both sexes are light- to mid-brown in colour but always look darker when they're wet.

This animal lives in the cool waters of the northern Pacific, frequenting beaches and rocky coastlines inshore. It ranges from north California to Alaska, across the Bering Sea to Russia's Kamchatka Peninsula and as far south as northern Japan. In the 1970s its total population was thought to be around 280,000, with 85% in Alaska. There has since been a startling decline, with the Alaskan population falling by more than half.

Baywatch bulls

Although lumbering on land, Steller's sea-lions become torpedo-like hunters beneath the waves, pursuing a wide variety of open-water fish, squid and octopus.

During the breeding season large numbers congregate at traditional beach 'rookeries' that are very noisy and smelly. Males arrive first and try to stake their territorial claims. Once a prime spot is won, they won't leave their position for fear of losing it to a rival, so cannot feed throughout the entire breeding season.

Females arrive in late spring or early summer and shortly afterwards give birth to a single pup, becoming ready to mate again just four days later. A dominant bull or 'beach master' aggressively guards up to 30 mated females. But remarkably, though their eggs are fertilised, the females delay implantation and so do not become properly pregnant until October.

A week or so after having her pup the mother is back out to sea fishing. Most pups are weaned at around one year, but may continue suckling for two to three years. Both males and females become sexually mature at three to six years, but males rarely breed successfully until eight to ten years when they're big enough to defend a territory.

WHERE TO SEE IT

The shores of Queen Charlotte Island off the coast of British Columbia are good sites: Duff Rock in Fife Sound is a favoured basking spot and wildlife cruises regularly visit the area, May to October being the best time. Other renowned spots lie around Vancouver Island: Norris Rocks near Hornby Island and Race Rocks near Victoria. In Alaska you may well see them on cruises into Glacier Bay National Park and especially around Brothers Island in Frederick Sound. Across the Pacific you can see them around the Commander Islands off Kamchatka, Russia.

THREATS

The dramatic decline of this species in the last quarter of a century is still puzzling. Possible causes include pollution, over fishing, disease and parasites, increased disturbance at rookeries and even predation by orcas.

303
EDGE RANK

Blue whale

Balaenoptera musculus

Total length: 24–29m; Weight: 120–170 tonnes

Leviathan

It's difficult to imagine a mammal, like ourselves, the size of a plane. But that's exactly what the blue whale is: the biggest animal ever to have existed. Its torpedo-like shape culminates in a massive flat-topped head that accommodates the cavernous mouth. Hanging from the upper jaw are 300–400 furry, comb-like structures called baleen plates, which act like giant curtains to filter food from great gulps of seawater.

Blue whales are greyish-blue in colour with light grey mottling above and a low (only 33cm) dorsal fin. Around 90 grooves extend from the chin and throat to the navel, and expand dramatically when feeding. The towering blow (or spout) is the highest of any whale, reaching up to 9m.

These immense creatures inhabit the open oceans in both cold and temperate waters, and often prefer the edge of continental shelves. They occur in the Arctic, Atlantic, Indian and Pacific oceans, from the tropics to the drift-ice of polar waters. It is thought that only 5,000 or so remain.

Food for thought

This species migrates over vast distances, spending the summer feeding in high latitude regions (towards the poles) and returning to warmer tropical waters in the winter for mating and calving. As the seasons are reversed in the northern and southern hemispheres, populations that migrate to each do so at different times of the year and so remain separate.

Blue whales are usually seen alone or in small groups, although aggregations of up to 60 may form in areas of plentiful food. They consume vast quantities of shrimp-like crustaceans called krill, by gulping in large amounts of water and then forcing this out with their tongue through the baleen, leaving the krill trapped in the fibres. In areas where feeding is good they may eat 3,600kg of krill each day – the weight of an elephant. Most feeding occurs at less than 100m depth, with dives lasting 10–20 minutes. Away from summer feeding grounds the whales fast, surviving on stored fat.

Once in their warmer water wintering grounds, females give birth to a single calf (rarely twins) after a gestation period of around 10–12 months. These are born 7m long and weighing around two tonnes. Fuelled by their mother's rich milk, they grow astonishingly fast, putting on 90kg per day until they are weaned after seven to eight months, by which time they are about 15m long. Small calves may be vulnerable to orcas, but adults have no natural predators. Sexual maturity is reached at five to ten years. Blue whales can live for 80 years or even longer.

Fin whale

Balaenoptera physalus

Total length: 19–24m; Weight: 70–80 tonnes

WHERE TO SEE IT

Whale watching in west Cork, Ireland, is now highly regarded. Family groups are resident from June until January. Details at: www.whalewatchwestcork.com. The Bay of Biscay also produces regular sightings, including from car ferries between the UK and Spain. UK information at: www.seawatchfoundation.org.uk. During summer (June to September) fin whales are frequently observed in the Gulf of Maine, the Bay of Fundy, the Gulf of St Lawrence and off Nova Scotia. Sanguenay Fjord and the surrounding waters of the Gulf of St Lawrence is a renowned spot: you can approach them on boats and in kayaks.

THREATS

Initially ignored by whalers because of its speed, modern technologies later brought the fin whale within range of commercial hunting. Blubber, oil and baleen were highly prized, and from 1946 to 1965 over 30,000 individuals were killed every year. Even though whaling bans have since allowed recovery, Populations still suffer from pollution and collisions with boats.

=88 EDGE RANK

Greyhound of the sea

The fin whale is a smaller version of the blue whale, not that the second-largest animal on the planet could ever be described as 'small'. It derives its name from the prominent curved dorsal fin that reaches up to 60cm. This whale is remarkable for two reasons: it is the fastest of all whales, with a top speed of nearly 40km/h earning it the soubriquet 'greyhound of the sea'; and it is able to leap (breach) clear of the water.

Fin whales are grey above and white below, with asymmetrical patterns on the jaw. In common with other rorquals (Norwegian for 'furrow whale'), they have a large number of grooves extending from the throat to the naval.

This species lives in both coastal waters and open oceans. Its global distribution covers the Atlantic, Pacific, Indian and Arctic oceans, though it rarely frequents tropical or iced polar seas. It is the only rorqual whale that commonly enters the western Mediterranean Sea.

Filter feeders

Like blue whales, fin whales spend spring and early summer in cold water feeding grounds at higher latitudes, then migrate to warmer waters for winter. This means that different populations from the two hemispheres never meet.

These whales usually occur in pairs or small 'pods' of about six or seven individuals. Larger groups of up to 300 have occasionally been observed. They feed by filtering crustaceans, fish and squid through their baleen, diving to depths of up to 230m and remaining submerged for about 15 minutes. Their blow reaches 6m.

Breeding takes place in winter, and a female generally returns to the same wintering quarters year on year. She produces a single calf, which she suckles for six to seven months and which accompanies her as she travels to the summer feeding grounds the following season.

Sperm whale

Physeter catodon

Total length: 11–20m (males); 10–17m (females)
Weight: 25–45 tonnes

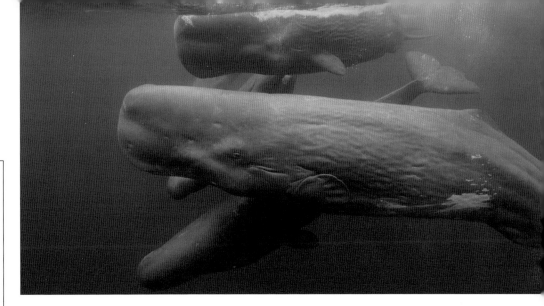

WHERE TO SEE IT

Kaikoura on New Zealand's South Island is hard to beat. Boat trips run most days and you can also take aerial viewing flights: http://www.whales.co.nz. Another 'hotspot' is the Sea of Cortez: www.bajawhales.com; home.btconnect.com/wildwings/baja.html. The Caribbean off Dominica is home to sperm whales year-round, with November to March being best: www.avirtualdominica.com/divingdominica.cfm

THREATS

People have exploited sperm whales for centuries. Large-scale hunting began in the north Atlantic in the early 1700s for spermaceti and ambergris (a substance found in the whales' stomach), both of which were used in the perfume and cosmetics industry. Commercial whaling has since stopped, but smaller scale exploitation continues in places. Further threats include entanglement in deep-sea fishing gear and accidental collisions with boats.

109
EDGE RANK

A sea of superlatives

If brain size measured intelligence, this species – with the largest brain on the planet – would have a formidable intellect. Little wonder that Melville pitted a clever sperm whale against the obsessive Captain Ahab in *Moby Dick*. Furthermore, this is the biggest toothed whale, the world's largest predatory animal and it dives deeper than any other creature.

Sperm whales have dark brown or blackish skin, a humped and knobbly spine and a huge square head that takes up almost a third of their length. Males may be three times larger than females. The head is often scarred from battles with prey and has a single blowhole on the left that produces a low, balloon-like spout.

A large cavity in the head contains a waxy liquid called spermaceti oil, which is believed to help with the whales' echolocation. Early whalers misinterpreted the origin of this oily substance – hence the species' name.

Sperm whales inhabit the open ocean, but may appear in deep waters inshore. They occur in all of the world's oceans, except the high Arctic. Males travel vast distances between polar feeding grounds and warm water breeding areas.

Dive, dive, dive

Early mariners hearing clicking sounds through the hull assumed these came from something they called 'carpenter fish'. In fact they were the sound of sperm whales using echolocation to find their prey, mostly giant squid, octopuses and fish. In pursuit of this food, sperm whales can hold their breath for nearly two hours and reach depths of a staggering 2,000m, perhaps more.

Adult females live with immature animals of both sexes in nursery groups. Bulls leave at maturity to join bachelor groups. Older bulls visit nursery groups to mate with cows during the breeding season. Females mature at 7–11 years; males do not begin to breed until they approach 20. A single calf is born after a gestation period of around 16 months and suckles for up to two years. Females in nursery herds are highly protective and, if threatened, will encircle the calves in a defensive formation with their tails facing outward.

Blue planet: the world of ocean

Dr Bernard Stonehouse

Atlantic, Indian, Pacific, Arctic, Southern: we divide the world ocean into separate basins, under names created mainly for our convenience. But there is in fact just one ocean, a single watery mantle spread around the world and fringed by dozens of coastal seas and bays. Beyond its continental shores lie narrow, sloping shelves, then steeper slopes to the wide floors of the main ocean basins, where mountain ranges and narrow trenches create a submarine topography every bit as varied as that on land. Within the ocean there is life at every level – much of it, from whales to periwinkles, concentrated near the surface and on the shores, shelves and slopes, with just a thin scattering on the deep ocean floor.

This submarine world has long intimidated humans, who have learned to traverse the ocean and harvest its abundant riches with little understanding of what lies beneath. We now know that systems within the oceans are fundamental to life on our planet. From their vast surface, water evaporates into the air, condensing to fall as rain and snow. It gathers into lakes, streams and rivers, returning to the oceans with a burden of dissolved gases, minerals and sediments. Within them huge masses of water circulate and stream, driven upward, down and sideways by winds, gravity and Earth's rotation. Water melting from icebergs off the coast of Antarctica may disappear into the depths, to emerge at the surface off Peru or West Africa, and continue in ever-circling currents to the high Arctic.

Voyages of discovery

For land-based humans, exploring the oceans has always been a dangerous business. Yet sea-going boats were in use well over 15,000 years ago. By the 3rd millennium BC European traders were navigating the Mediterranean and Aegean seas, well out of sight of land, and Polynesians were exploring wide expanses of the island-strewn Pacific Ocean. By the mid-13th century much of the Mediterranean was charted, and Viking adventurers had found their way across the open ocean to Iceland, Greenland and North America. In the 15th and 16th centuries two- and three-masted sailing ships, using the simplest navigational instruments and techniques, explored in turn the Atlantic, Pacific and Indian oceans, establishing beyond doubt that the world was not only round, but well worth exploring for its raw materials and trade goods.

▲ *Viking longboats, from Historical Tales, The Romance of Reality, Charles Morris, 1893*

We know of the ships that returned successfully to their home ports. Many others did not, usually for reasons that were never discovered. Shipwreck apart, the most serious hazard on long sea voyages was scurvy, a disease caused by a deficiency of vitamin C, which destroyed entire ships' companies. We know too of tall tales brought back after long months at sea – of hurricanes, giant waves, ice islands and sea monsters, including some that may well have been true, for all of these are still reported today.

▲ *Earth seen from space, as captured by NASA's Terra satellite.*

While sailors and passengers could afford to be fanciful, navigators and scientists could not. The twin sciences of oceanography and marine biology began with the painstaking work of 18th and 19th century scientific expeditions. Notable among them were the world voyages of James Cook (1768-80), George Vancouver (1795), Thaddeus von Bellingshausen (1819-21) and the long voyage of HMS *Challenger* (1872–76) to study deep-sea circulation and the ocean floor. These expeditions carried scientists and observers who disclosed not only the diversity of ocean life, but its incredible wealth in parts of the world where currents brought nutrients to surface waters. Cook, who was first to identify and explore the Southern Ocean, together with early Arctic explorers, noted particularly the summer abundance of birds, seals and whales in cold polar waters, giving rise to some of the world's most profitable and lasting fisheries.

Getting down to it

How do we explore the ocean bed? In 1943 The French oceanographer Jacques-Yves Cousteau pioneered the aqualung for scuba-diving, a lightweight underwater breathing apparatus that allows swimmers to descend freely to about 30m – deep enough to explore coral reefs. This, for the first time, enabled scientists to observe the behaviour of marine creatures under water. Deeper down, however, humans need protection from the great pressure of water. Bathyscaphes (strong metal chambers with windows, lights and cameras, built to withstand enormous pressures), were invented and developed by the Belgian underwater explorers Auguste and Jacques Piccard, enabling them in 1960 to descend for the first time to over 10,000m in some of the ocean's deepest corners. They found marine animals living even at those great depths.

▲ Early whalers in pursuit of a bowhead whale (1849, artist unknown)

Those early expeditions explored oceans that were clean and as yet hardly affected by humans. Since their time an ever-expanding human population has raided the oceans for fish, seals and whales, criss-crossed them with busy shipping lanes, and polluted them with oil, industrial residues and plastic artefacts. Today scientists and navigators are still at work, on dedicated research ships of many nations, discovering new facts, new plants and animals, and new ways towards better management of the world's oceans.

▲ French oceanographer Jacques Cousteau (1910–1997), in an old diving suit (top) and in a French maritime museum in 1973 (above)

Background: Map showing the world's oceans according to Ortelius, AD 1570

Dr Bernard Stonehouse is a marine biologist with special interests in the ecology of seabirds and mammals. He has published many research papers and several books covering both tropical and polar research.

Polar bear

Ursus maritimus

Head/body length: 2.0–2.6m (male); 1.8–2.1m (female)
Height at shoulder: 1.5–1.7m
Weight: 400–600kg, (males); 200–350kg (females)

Great white hunter

No creature symbolises the frozen Arctic wilderness
more than the polar bear, which has been revered
for centuries by the indigenous peoples of the
Arctic. The Inuit call it *Nanuk* and consider it to be
wise, powerful and 'almost a man'.

This massive, unmistakable predator is the largest
land carnivore, weighing twice as much as a
Siberian tiger. Only its pads and the tip of its nose
are not covered in fur. Powerful forelimbs and huge
forepaws act like paddles when swimming, and
heavy claws help dig through snow and ice.

On thin ice

This bear lives wherever ice forms annually around the coast and there are plenty of seals and other prey. Its range is limited by the extent of sea ice, but covers the circumpolar Arctic from Canada to Alaska, Greenland, Spitsbergen and northern Russia. Twenty known subpopulations occur, with little or no mingling or interbreeding.

The southernmost limit is James Bay in Canada at about the same latitude as London. During cold winters, when ice creeps further south, individuals may move as far south as Newfoundland and into the northern Bering Sea. With the ice caps retreating due to global warming, however, so is the polar bear's range. Current estimates put the total population at around 20,000–25,000.

Seal of approval

Polar bears have a remarkable sense of smell: they can sniff out a seal's breathing hole, concealed beneath a metre of ice and snow, from nearly a kilometre. Ringed and bearded seals are favourite prey, caught as they surface to breathe.

More opportunistically they may take on walruses, belugas and narwhals, and will scavenge whale carcasses and other carrion.

Most feeding occurs in just three months between April and July when seal pups are abundant. At such times polar bears can polish off huge amounts of food at astonishing speed. If food is not available, however, they can slow their metabolism right down to conserve resources. In extreme conditions they may fast for six months or more.

For most of the year polar bears are solitary, although adults may congregate at preferred sights during the enforced summer fast. They are excellent swimmers and have been seen in open Arctic waters as far as 90km from land. Some individuals spend as much as half of their lives on ice floes, effectively making them sea mammals.

Breeding takes place from late March to late May and a pair remains together for one to two weeks to ensure a successful mating. Cubs are born in a snow den in December and January. They remain dependent on their mother for 2.5 years, so she is only able to mate once every three years.

WHERE TO SEE IT

Churchill, on the shores of Hudson Bay in Manitoba, Canada, is the self-proclaimed polar bear capital of the world. Bears congregate here annually and are particularly abundant in October and November as they wait for the pack ice to form. Bear watching is from purpose-built tundra buggies, and there are several local lodges and numerous tour operators. Further afield in Manitoba, Nanuk and Watchee lodges offer polar bear viewing in more remote and secluded surroundings. Spitsbergen, in Norway's Svalbard Archipelago, is another renowned location and several operators offer cruises. Details at: www.polarbearsinternational.org

THREATS

At present polar bear numbers are reasonably healthy. However, climate change could alter this in the blink of an eye. If global warming continues at present rates, the ice caps will melt and polar bears will no longer have a home. Already there are worrying signs in some areas, where winter ice fails to form and polar bears starve before they get a chance to feed. Pollutants that build up along the food chain are also a worry: being the apex carnivores, the bears suffer from 'bio-accumulation' with magnified toxin levels causing various detrimental effects.

493
EDGE RANK

Dugong

Dugong dugon

Total length: 240–330cm; Weight: 230–600kg

WHERE TO SEE IT

Australia's Great Barrier Reef Marine Park is home to an estimated 14,000 dugongs and there are 16 protected areas along the Queensland coast for these creatures. In Western Australia, Monkey Mia in Shark Bay and Ningaloo Reef Marine Park are good locations. Dimakya Island, near Palawan in the Philippines, is also renowned for observing dugongs in their natural habitat: divers and non-divers alike can take tours along the coast to find the animals, and sometimes even snorkel with them. Details at: www.clubparadise palawan.com/dugongwatch.htm

THREATS

This species was long hunted for its meat, hide, oil and bones. Although commercial hunting is now banned, dugong products are still highly valued. In some areas of Australia and the Torres Straits, traditional hunting continues. Habitat loss is also a major threat, as sea grass ecosystems are very sensitive to disturbance. Entanglement in fishing nets and direct hits by boats also cause numerous deaths.

53
EDGE RANK

Mermaid myth

This strange creature has human-like breasts and may well have spawned myths of mermaids. It is descended from land mammals that browsed in shallow grassy swamps 60 million years ago. And remarkably its closest living relative remains a land mammal: the elephant.

Dugongs are large and torpedo-shaped, with paddle-like flippers. They differ from closely related manatees (see page 138) in their fluked, dolphin-like tail. Their thick skin is smooth and brownish-grey, and their broad snout has huge muscular lips that curtain the relatively small mouth.

Dugongs are more strictly marine than manatees. They frequent shallow, tropical coasts across the Indo-Pacific region with an abundance of sea grass. Pockets survive in coastal waters from East Africa to Vanuatu in the western Pacific, but the largest numbers are in northern Australian waters. Here the population of around 80,000 may constitute more than half the global total.

Grass is greener

Dugongs are exclusively herbivorous and feed mainly on sea grass, hence their alternative name of 'sea-cow'. The ebb and flow of the tide determines their daily movements: they rest in deeper water until the sea grass beds are submerged and they can move inshore to feed. These slow-moving creatures have a low metabolism and cannot hold their breath for longer than about three minutes.

Herds of dugongs once numbered thousands. Being less abundant, this no longer happens, although groups of a hundred or more may appear on good feeding grounds. Otherwise, they usually occur alone or in pairs.

Breeding appears to take place throughout the year, with females producing a single calf after 13–14 months gestation. Calves are born in the shallows and surface immediately to take their first breath. They begin eating sea grass at around three months but also continue to suckle until 11–15 months. Dugongs may live more than 70 years in the wild.

Beluga

Delphinapterus leucas

Total length: 3.7–5.5m (males); 3.0–4.1m (females)
Weight: 500–1,500kg

Whiter than white

Looking like rafts of giant white maggots, a large gathering of belugas is a strange sight. These blizzard-white whales have an oddly undersized head, and a stocky but streamlined body. Youngsters are born grey, gradually becoming whiter with age.

Unlike most dolphins and whales, belugas lack a dorsal fin: indeed their scientific name '*Delphinapterus*' means 'dolphin-without-a-wing'. Other features include a flexible neck that can turn the head through nearly 90 degrees and flexible lips that produce a variety of facial expressions. Their thick blubber constitutes up to 80% of body weight and provides excellent insulation.

Belugas live in freezing Arctic waters, usually around the ice edge. They spend summer in shallow bays and estuaries and retreat to the pack ice in winter. Their range takes in northern Russia, North America, Greenland and Svalbard. Most populations migrate north in spring then move south in the autumn once the ice starts to form.

Sea songster

Belugas produce a variety of sounds, including moos, grunts, chirps and whistles. These are audible through the hulls of ships and the beluga was nicknamed 'sea canary' by early Arctic sailors. In fact the sounds are emitted from the nasal passages and are used to detect prey by echolocation.

Prey includes a variety of fish, crustaceans and worms, most of which live on the seabed. The flexible lips act like a vacuum cleaner and suck prey into the mouth. Although belugas spend most of the time at the surface, they make regular dives of 1,000m or more to feed.

In summer, thousands gather in estuaries. Females and calves tend to stick together while males form

bachelor groups. They often moult at this time and can be seen rubbing off the previous year's withered yellow skin in the shallows.

Females mature at four to seven years. A single calf is born after a gestation period of around 11 months. The mother–calf bond is very strong: the calf continues to suckle well into its second year and the pair are inseparable.

When trapped by the ice, belugas may fall prey to orcas and polar bears.

Conserving wildlife in the world's oceans

Seventy per cent of the Earth's surface is a continuous body of water. Humans are land animals, however, and in managing Earth, we tend to look after the quarter that we know best, dismissing the oceans as little more than a source of fish and a dumping ground for rubbish. But that, we are finding, is a mistake. Oceans are no less important than land and need the same degree of management for their protection. As repositories for carbon dioxide and other greenhouse gases, they may hold the key to all our welfare. The consequences of events taking place anywhere in the world's oceans can ripple across the entire planet at startling speed.

Gone fishing

For millennia coastal people have caught sea fishes to eat. In a familiar pattern, as methods of harvesting have become more sophisticated, so subsistence gathering has evolved into commercial enterprise. Evidence has begun to mount that in many places this level of exploitation is no longer sustainable: not only do stocks of specific species collapse, but also their predators' numbers begin to fall and the whole ocean ecology is disrupted. The Marine Stewardship Council (*www.msc.org*) is an independent international organisation dedicated to raising consumer awareness of the issues surrounding overfishing and awards its certification to products from sustainably managed fisheries.

Giant killing

Whaling is a conservation issue that has been in the public eye for decades. Several nations have traditionally hunted whales, with a growing impact upon the animals' populations as demand increased. Many species – including the blue whale, the world's largest-ever animal – were hunted to the brink of extinction during the 19th and early 20th centuries. In 1982 the 77 members of the International Whaling Commission (www.iwcoffice.org) agreed to cease hunting all whale species after 1985. However, several countries, including Norway, Iceland and Japan, have defied the moratorium by continuing to hunt minke whales and other species, some under the guise of scientific research, and are pressuring the IWC to allow the resumption of large-scale whaling. The environmental activist organisation Greenpeace (www.greenpeace.org) is heavily involved in opposing these moves, pointing out that the slow reproduction rate of whales means that some species remain endangered despite not being hunted for 40 years.

▲ *Blood money: Whaling continues in several countries, despite a worldwide ban.*

▲ *Net losses: The fishing industry is responsible for the deaths of many non-target species, like this great white shark.*

WHALE WATCHING GUIDELINES
www.ngo.grida.no/wwfap/whalewatching/iwc_guidelines.shtml

It is not just the fisheries' target species that are at risk. Certain modern fishing methods, such as trawl netting, catch significant numbers of non-target species too, most notoriously cetaceans. Oceania (*www.oceania.org*), an organisation that campaigns to protect and restore the world's oceans, states that for the 80–100 million tonnes of fish harvested annually by industrial fishing worldwide, 27 million tonnes is discarded as 'bycatch' – including a shocking 300,000 marine mammals. The European Cetacean Bycatch Campaign (*www.eurocbc.org*) is another body that campaigns for fisheries to take measures to reduce their level of cetacean bycatch.

Poisoned water

When oil tankers leak their load, the impact upon marine wildlife is often distressingly obvious. However, oil and other pollutants released from sea vessels accounts for only 12% of marine pollution. Nearly half of all sea contamination originates on land, in such forms as sewage, agricultural run-off and industrial waste. So-called 'nutrient pollution' from agricultural waste and sewage can foster the development of algal blooms, which deoxygenate coastal water, killing other marine life. More insidiously, some chemical toxins accumulate in marine animals' body tissues, becoming more concentrated as they travel up the food chain.

Research has shown that the bodies of ringed seals in the Baltic contain excessively high levels of PCBs (polychlorinated biphenyls), part of the group of toxins known as persistent organic pollutants (POPs). PCBs are widely used in a variety of industries although their manufacture is now banned in many countries, and they are apparently the cause of serious reproductive problems in the seals. Polar bears across the Arctic Circle show similarly high levels of PCBs. The World Wildlife Fund (*www.wwf.org*) is involved in lobbying governments around the world to sign up to the Stockholm POPs Convention, which aims to control and eventually eradicate the use of POPs.

Oceans and climate

Pollution, in its atmospheric form, is also a key factor in global warming, which is now being felt across the world's oceans through such effects as melting ice sheets, dying coral and coastal flooding. Polar Bears International (*www.polarbearsinternational.org*) identifies global warming as the key threat to this species and others that depend on polar ice. Warming oceans further south are also thought to have affected the distribution of the lesser sand eel, leading to disastrous breeding failure in seabirds, such as

puffins, that depend upon this species for food. The Earthwatch Institute (*www.earthwatch.org*) is recruiting volunteers for a number of expeditions investigating global warming in the Arctic and elsewhere.

The effects of global warming on the oceans may have even further-reaching consequences. The oceans help control our climate: they store heat energy and transport it in currents around the world, providing a buffer against climate change and influencing weather conditions on land. Thus we and all other land animals depend upon healthy oceans to survive. While what goes on miles under the sea's surface may be out of sight, we cannot afford for it to be out of mind.

▲ *Flotsam and jetsam:* Discarded fishing material is a hazard for marine creatures, such as this Atlantic fur seal. ▲ *Surface damage:* Pelicans and other seabirds are at particular risk from spilt oil and other floating pollutants. ▲ *On thin ice:* Thanks to global warming, the polar bear's habitat is literally disappearing from beneath its feet.

Conservation Contacts

ARKive (*www.arkive.org*) A website with an ark of media material about endangered species, including information, photos and films.

Conservation International (*2011 Crystal Dr, Suite 500, Arlington, Virginia 2220, USA; www.conservation.org*) Works on projects worldwide that adopt a highly focused approach, concentrating on biodiversity hotspots.

David Shepherd Wildlife Foundation (*61 Smithbrook Kilns, Cranleigh, Surrey GU6 8JJ; www.davidshepherd.org or www.artforsurvival.org*) Founded by the famous wildlife artist, DSWF is non-bureaucratic and effective, funding long-term projects in Africa and Asia to save tigers, rhinos, elephants and other critically endangered mammals in the wild. Raises funds through subscription, donation and art-based events.

Durrell Wildlife Conservation Trust (*Les Augrès Manor, La Profonde Rue, Trinity, Jersey JE3 5BP, Channel Islands; www.durrellwildlife.org*) Founded by the famous writer and conservationist Gerald Durrell, this organisation works specifically with endangered species (often the less glamorous ones) and has strong in-country education and staff training programmes.

EDGE of Existence (*www.edgeofexistence.org*) a recent initiative from the Zoological Society of London. EDGE stands for Evolutionarily Distinct and Globally Endangered and aims to highlight the plight of unusual species at risk of extinction.

IUCN: World Conservation Union (*Rue Mauverney 28, Gland 1196, Switzerland; www.iucn.org*) The world's largest conservation network, it aims to influence, encourage and assist societies throughout the world to conserve the integrity and diversity of nature, and to ensure the equitable and ecologically sustainable use of natural resources.

IUCN Red List of Threatened Species (*www.iucnredlist.org*) The International Union for Conservation of Nature and Natural Resources' official red list of threatened species.

Save the Rhino International (*16 Winchester Wlk, London SE1 9AQ; www.savetherhino.org*) Works to conserve wild populations of critically endangered rhinos. Famous for its fundraising events (eg: city marathons) with rhino costumes. Makes grants to rhino- and community-based conservation projects in Africa and Asia.

The Orang-utan Foundation UK (*7 Kent Terr, London NW1 4RP; www.orangutan.org.uk*) Supports repatriation and wild orang-utan conservation work in Indonesia and Malaysia. Seeks to advise government policy and educate the public about orang-utans, other fauna and flora and their habitats. Raises funds and awareness in the UK and overseas.

TRAFFIC International (*219a Huntingdon Rd, Cambridge CB3 ODL; www.wwfmalaysia.org or www.traffic.org*) Tackling illegal trade in endangered species, including their parts and products.

Whale and Dolphin Conservation Society (*Brookfield Hse, 38 St Paul St, Chippenham, Wiltshire SN15 1LJ; www.wdcs.org*) A global voice for the protection of whales, dolphins and their environment. The world's most active charity dedicated to the conservation and welfare of cetaceans.

Wildlife Conservation Society (*2300 Southern Blvd, Bronx, New York 10460, USA; www.wcs.org*) An international organisation based at the Bronx Zoo that works to save wildlife and wild lands through careful science, international conservation, education and resource management.

World Wide Fund for Nature (WWF) International (*Gland Av du Mont Blanc, 1196 Gland, Switzerland; www.wwf.org or www.panda.org*) Established in 1961, WWF operates in more than 100 countries working for a future in which humans live in harmony with nature. WWF currently funds around 2,000 conservation projects around the world.

Zoological Society of London (ZSL) (*Outer Circle, Regent's Pk, London NW1 4RY; www.zsl.org*). Encompasses London and Whipsnade Zoos and is at the forefront of research and field-based conservation, including EDGE (see above).

Acknowledgements

In late March this year, I innocently strolled into the Bradt office to chat about a new edition of *Madagascar Wildlife*. An hour later, I left having agreed to write a completely different book and to do so in an unprecedented short space of time. Such is the urgency when dealing with endangered animals.

However, a daunting task was made bearable and achievable by the help and enthusiasm of others, without whom I'd have sunk without trace.

My thanks extend to Donald Greig, whose initial brainchild this title was. From the outset his unshakable commitment has inspired confidence and calm. Similarly, the rest of the team at Bradt – Daniel Austin, Emma Thomson, Caroline Mardall and Helen Anjomshoaa – have thrown their heart and soul into the project.

Mike Unwin's rigorous editorial guidance helped maintain my focus and provide direction throughout. I am also grateful for his many significant contributions to the text, both in shaping my words and adding many of his own.

At the outset discussions with Dr Jonathan Baillie and Carly Waterman from the EDGE of Existence project provided valuable insight, while Caroline George, also at the Zoological Society of London has been enthusiastic and supportive.

I am indebted to Laura Barwick who helped with chunks of research. Even when swamped with other deadlines, she answered eleventh-hour SOS calls and delivered every time. Her snippets on Skype were a warming and welcome distraction, as were updates on the test match score. Thanks also to Mark Carwardine and Tom Walmsley for useful information on best places to see some species.

My final and fondest thank you goes to Hilary, the founder of Bradt Travel Guides. She and I are bonded by our fondness for and frustration with Madagascar. Hilary gave me a helping hand into the treacherous world of book writing and published my first efforts. She has repeatedly encouraged and supported my work, and her enthusiasm for travel, the natural world and life in general is naïve, heartening and infectious.

It was a quirk of timing that a month before she handed over the reins of the charming publishing empire she had created, this project was conceived. Despite the tight timeframe, she convinced me it was possible. I hope the finished product does justice to Hilary's loyalty and vision and I wish her a long, happy and very adventurous retirement.

Nick Garbutt – August 2007

It was a great pleasure working with Nick and the Bradt team against the clock in bringing this exciting project to fruition. Sobering, also, that our number one species – the Yangtze river dolphin – hit the headlines as 'probably extinct' just as we went to press. I wholeheartedly reiterate Nick's thanks to all the Bradt team for their support and hard work. Many thanks also to Chris Lane and the team at Artinfusion for their excellent design work, and to all the additional writers who at short notice provided the fascinating individual essays on history and conservation, namely Hilary Bradt, Philip Briggs, Andrew Evans, Stella Martin, Gehan de Silva Wijeyeratne, Dr Bernard Stonehouse, Marianne Taylor and Martin Walters. Finally, I'd like to thank my parents for inspiring my love of wildlife in the first place, my wife Kathy, for all her support and editorial wisdom, and my daughter Florence for keeping my eyes open to the natural world.

Mike Unwin – August 2007

Picture credits

Index

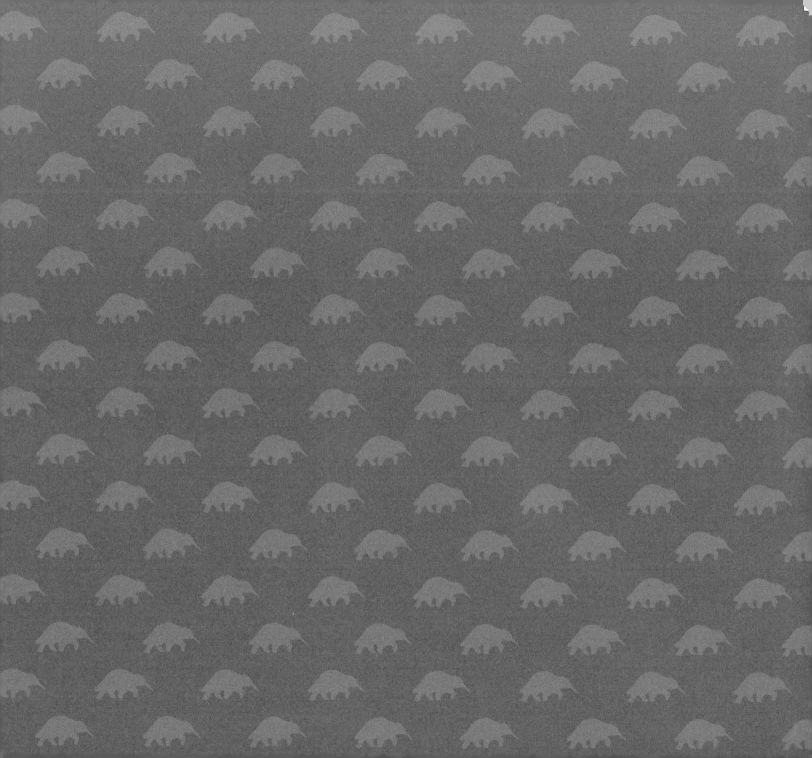